ALCHEMY
AND
KABBALAH

Published by Spring Publications, Inc.
www.springpublications.com

Originally published in German under the title *Alchemie und Kabbala*
in *Eranos Yearbook* 46 (1977). Subsequently included in G. Scholem,
Judaica 4, ed. R. Tiedemann. Frankfurt am Main: Suhrkamp Verlag, 1984.

Inquiries should be addressed to:
Spring Publications, Inc.
P.O. Box 230212
New York, N.Y. 10023

First Edition 2006
Second, revised printing 2008

Design: white.room productions, New York

Printed in Canada

Copy editor: Michaelyn Mitchell

Library of Congress Cataloging-in-Publication Data

Scholem, Gershom Gerhard, 1897-
  [Alchemie und kabbala. English]
  Alchemy and kabbalah / translated from the German by Klaus Ottmann.— 1st ed.
     p. cm.
  Includes bibliographical references and index.
  ISBN-13: 978-0-88214-566-2 (pbk. original : alk. paper)
  ISBN-10: 0-88214-566-5 (pbk. original : alk. paper)
  1. Cabala—History. 2. Alchemy. I. Ottmann, Klaus. II. Title.

BM526.S34813 2006

296.1'6—dc22

                          2006002853

♾ The paper used in this publication meets the minimum requirements of the
American National Standard for Information Sciences—Permanence of Paper for
Printed Library Materials, ANSI Z39.48-1992.

GERSHOM SCHOLEM

ALCHEMY AND KABBALAH

Translated from the German
by Klaus Ottmann

SPRING PUBLICATIONS
PUTNAM, CONN.

Perspective diagram of the ten *sefirot,* composed of the initial
letters of the names of each *sefirah*, with the first, *Keter,* being the
outermost, from Moses Cordovero's *Pardes Rimmonim* (Cracow, 1592)

CONTENTS

Alchemy and Kabbalah

TRANSLATOR'S NOTE

In translating biblical citations, I have relied on the *Tanakh: The Holy Scriptures. The New JPS Translation According to the Traditional Hebrew Text* (Philadelphia and Jerusalem: Jewish Publication Society, 1985). This volume has also been my guide for the transliteration of the names of biblical figures. Citations from the *Zohar* are, wherever possible, taken from the ongoing translation by Daniel C. Matt, *The Zohar: Pritzker Edition* (Stanford Univ. Press, 2004 ff.). In regard to the transliteration of Hebrew names and titles of Hebraic works I have followed, for the most part, the *Encyclopædia Judaica* (Jerusalem and New York, 1971–72), including certain concessions made by the editors of the *Encyclopædia* that are based on usage (e.g., *mitzvah* rather than *miẓvah*).

This second printing contains minor revisions and corrections. I thank Karljürgen G. Feuerherm of the Department of Archaeology and Classical Studies at Wilfrid Laurier University, Waterloo, Ontario, for his valuable suggestions.

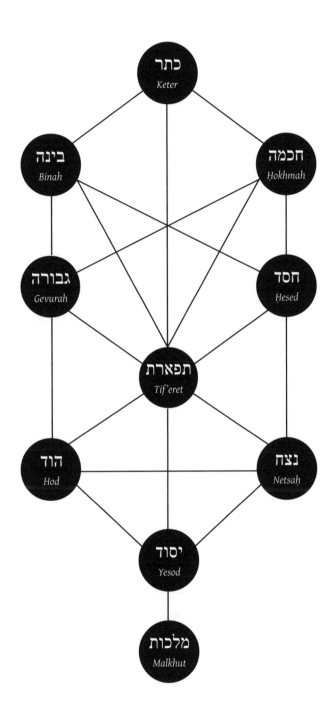

The ten *Sefirot*

T here is some benefit to be had from youthful courage and perhaps even from foolishness. Some fifty years ago, in one of my first large studies on the Kabbalah,[1] I wrote about this subject, and now, more learned and perhaps wiser, although coming to the end of my career, I am embarking on it once again in order to develop it further. In doing so, I certainly will refer here and there to that youthful study; however, the perspective I have gained since that time diverges significantly from my earlier approach. Moreover, there is much new material at my disposal.

G. S.

---

1 G. Scholem, "Alchemie und Kabbala. Ein Kapitel aus der Geschichte der Mystik," *Monatsschrift für Geschichte und Wissenschaft des Judentums* 69 (1925): 13–30; 95–110.

I

Ever since the end of the Middle Ages, when the European world became acquainted with Jewish mysticism and theosophy, the Kabbalah has been thought of as a complex intertwining of a multitude of concepts. The name of this arcane discipline became a popular catchword in Renaissance and Baroque theosophical and occult circles, having been declared and revered as the guardian of the oldest and highest mystical wisdom of mankind by its first Christian mediators, among them, Giovanni Pico della Mirandola and Johannes Reuchlin. Since there was nothing to be feared from the very few who were knowledgeable about the real Kabbalah, it became a kind of banner under which the public could be offered just about anything – from the authentically Jewish or weakly Judaic meditations of deeply Christian mystics to the carnival attractions of geomancy and tarot-card fortune-telling. The word Kabbalah stirred up reverential shudders and enveloped all. Even the most alien elements of occidental folklore became "Kabbalah"; even the natural sciences of the time, such as astrology, alchemy, and natural magic, were in some sense leaning toward occultism. Kabbalah continues to bear this heavy burden, one that at times obscures its true content – in the *communis opinio,* with lay and theosophical adepts, and in the language of many European writers and even scholars. In this century, with charlatans such as Aleister Crowley and his followers in England, and especially in the nineteenth century, with Éliphas Lévi, Papus (Gérard Encausse), and other French theosophists of the Martinist school, everything humanly possible has been done to confound all occult disciplines with the "sacred" Kabbalah. Many books that flaunt the word Kabbalah on their title pages have nothing or practically nothing to do with it.

It is important to separate those elements that historically belong or relate to the Kabbalah from those that have become confused with it by developments that run their course outside Judaism. To this latter group belongs the relation between alchemy and Kabbalah. For more than four hundred years, the terms alchemy and Kabbalah have been synonymous among the Christian theosophists and alchemists of Europe, so much so that one might suspect that there are strong internal connections. My purpose here is to explore this subject critically.

In the scientific discussion of the systematic relation between mysticism and alchemy (seemingly aimed at the purely scientific goal of the transmutation of metals into gold), there are two very different perspectives at work. One view, as expressed in the great works of E. von Lippmann and L. Thorndike, regards these relations from purely external, historical points of view.[2] Another view, asserted with growing insistence and influence, describes vast provinces of alchemy as de facto internal human processes. Since 1850 there have been comprehensive undertakings in this direction, based on an almost consistently symbolic interpretation of alchemical processes and the actions of its adepts toward an understanding of the internal "spiritual" life of mankind. Hence the object of alchemy is not the transformation of metals but that of mankind itself. The "philosophical gold" that is to be produced is the perfection of the soul – mankind in the mystical stage of rebirth or redemption. First developed with extraordinary erudition in Ireland and America in the works of M. A. Atwood

---

2 E. von Lippmann, *Entstehung und Ausbreitung der Alchemie* (Berlin, 1919–31); L. Thorndike, *A History of Magic and Experimental Science,* 4 vols. (London, 1923 ff.).

and E. A. Hitchcock, respectively, this view was adopted by H. Silberer,[3] a pupil of Freud's, who gave it a psychoanalytic foundation. Inspired by Silberer, C. G. Jung interpreted this concept of alchemy in terms of his archetype-based analytical psychology, advancing it in books that would become widely known and influential.[4]

To this day, it is a matter of debate as to when this psychological aspect of alchemy first arose, and I do not intend to render an opinion about it. It is undeniable, however, that some prophetic biblical passages, such as Isaiah 1:25, which compares the catharsis of Israel with the refining of metals, could suggest such trains of thought. The comparison of God with pure gold in Job 22:24–25 also played a major role among the later alchemists. In his book *The Secret Tradition of Alchemy*, published several years prior to C. G. Jung's writings, A. E. Waite deals in detail with the question of dating the mystical reinterpretation of alchemy. He dates the first such reinterpretation to the end of the Middle Ages. In any case, I would concede that, in all probability, a not insignificant share of famous alchemical texts, especially after Paracelsus's time, do not pursue chemical goals but rather are meant as instructions for the mystical work of mankind. With some authors one may also presume that they consciously had in mind a coincidence of chemical and mystical processes, which I take

---

3 M. A. Atwood, *A Suggestive Inquiry into the Hermetic Mystery* (London, 1850; new edition, Belfast, 1918); E. A. Hitchcock, *Remarks upon Alchemy and the Alchemists* (Boston, 1857); H. Silberer, *Probleme der Mystik und ihrer Symbolik* (Vienna, 1914), translated by S. E. Jelliffe as *Problems of Mysticism and Its Symbolism* (New York, 1917).

4 C. G. Jung, *Psychology and Alchemy,* Collected Works, trans. R. F. C. Hull (New York, 1953ff.), vol. 12; "*Psychology of Transference*," in *Practice of Psychotherapy*, Collected Works, vol. 16, which is explained by means of alchemical imagery; *Mysterium Coniunctionis: An Inquiry into the Separation and Synthesis of Psychic Opposites in Alchemy*, Collected Works, vol. 14. Cf. also A. Faivre, "Mystische Alchemie und geistige Hermeneutik," *Eranos Yearbook* 42 (1973), 323–56.

to be the case, above all, for the alchemists associated with the Rosicrucians. Here we are without a doubt dealing essentially with a mystical movement whose scientific tendencies are byproducts of their symbolism and symbolic practices. It is precisely in these circles that the identification of Kabbalah with alchemy has asserted itself most emphatically.[5]

Before we can follow the crossovers that lead from the Kabbalah in Christian disguise to alchemy, we must answer the following questions: What is the Kabbalah's relation to alchemy in its original sources, as a more or less uniform system of mystical symbolism in its classical evolution from no later than the twelfth century to about 1600? Was alchemy widespread enough among the Jews prior to or concurrent with the development of Kabbalah to influence the formation of kabbalist symbolism? How little was known with certainty is evident from a remark by as eminent an authority as M. Steinschneider, who as late as 1878 wrote: "To my knowledge, the Kabbalah teaches nothing about alchemy, even though it joined other superstitious disciplines."[6] Even as late as 1894, the same author wrote of a "lack of alchemical texts among Jews, which should be regarded as a virtue."[7]

At the same time, Steinschneider observed that "the Hebrew literature offers curiously little about the *magna ars*."[8] In

---

5 Éliphas Lévi's reversal of these relationships, whereby alchemy is but a "daughter of the Qabalah," has no validity; cf. his *The Key to the Great Mysteries*, trans. A. Crowley (London, 1959), 141.

6 *Jeschurun: Zeitschrift für die Wissenschaft des Judenthums* 9 (1878): 85.

7 *Monatsschrift für Geschichte und Wissenschaft des Judentums* 38 (1984): 42.

8 M. Steinschneider, *Die hebräischen Übersetzungen des Mittelalters* (Berlin, 1893), 273. Since then, three instructive articles on alchemy have been written: M. Gaster, in the *Jewish Encyclopedia* (New York, 1901–6), vol. 1, 328–32; B. Suler, in the German-language *Encyclopædia Judaica: Das Judentum in Geschichte und Gegenwart* (Berlin, 1928–34), vol. 2, cols. 137–59; and again B. Suler in

the older alchemical literature written in Greek – in the writings of Olympidor and Zosimos, for instance – Maria the Jewess (Maria Hebræa, Moses's sister)[9] and other Jews are indeed mentioned; however, these are pseudepigraphic, like most of the sources cited in this literature. The speculation advanced by some scholars that Zosimos, probably the most famous Greek alchemist of the fourth century, was a Jew is, as far as I can judge, not likely to be true.[10] However, in the eleventh century the Spanish Jew Moisés (Mosé) Sefardi, who became known as Petrus Alfonsi after his baptism, wrote a book whose content was revealed to Seth, the son of Adam, by the Angel Raziel, which describes, among other things, the transmutation of elements and metals.[11] Indeed, the classical Jewish

---

the revised English-language *Encyclopædia Judaica* (Jerusalem and New York, 1971–72), vol. 2, cols. 542–49.

9 On Maria the Jewess, see Lippmann, op. cit., 46. Lippmann declares that she was, without a doubt, Jewish since the following saying was attributed to her: "Do not touch [the Philosopher's Stone with your hands]: you are not of our stock, you are not of Abraham's bosom." This, of course, proves nothing since it could easily be part of the usual pseudoepigraphy. R. Eisler's defense of many of these fabrications is without substance; cf. his remarks in *Monatsschrift für Geschichte und Wissenschaft des Judentums* 69 (1925): 367.

10 J. Ruska, *Tabula Smaragdina* (Heidelberg, 1926), 41. Ruska also cites an Arabic source, where Zosimos is simply called "the Hebrew." The predilection of many alchemists for Jewish pseudoepigraphical authorities does not prove, as has sometimes been asserted, that Jews had a position of importance in ancient alchemy.

11 In the thirteenth century, Peter of Cornwall quotes this from a lost book by Petrus Alfonsi: "Est quidem liber apud Judeos de quo Petrus Alphonsi in libro suo quem appellavit *Humanum proficuum* loquitur discipulo suo querenti ab eo que essent nomina angelorum que invocata valerent ad mutandum ea *que ex elementis fiunt in alia et metalla in alia,* ita dicens: Hoc facillime potes scire si librum quem *secreta secretorum* appellant valeas invenire, quem sapientes Judei dicunt *Seth* filio Adam Rasielem angelum revelasse, atque angelorum nomina et dei precipua scripta esse." Cf. R.W. Hunt, "The Disputation of Peter of Cornwall against Symon the Jew," in *Studies*

philosophers mention alchemy only in passing and often deprecatorily. Judah Halevi dismissed the theories of "alchemists and pneumatists," who, in fact, often appear side by side in Arabic literature. Their experiments had misled them when they "believed to be able to measure off the elemental fire on their weighing scales to bring about arbitrary creations and mutate matter." [12] Similarly, Joseph Albo did not think much of false silver *(melekheth ha-alkimia)* produced by alchemy, which, when smelted, is revealed as fake. [13] The famous eleventh-century moralist Baḥya ben Joseph ibn Paquda expresses a more favorable opinion in the fourth chapter of his *Ḥovot ha-Levavot*, where he compares the tranquility of the soul with the efforts of the alchemists:

> Another advantage for him who relies on God is that he can free his mind from the affairs of the world and purify his soul for works of worship, so that in the peace of his mind and the tranquility of his soul, in his little concern with the affairs of this world, he is very like the master of alchemy who is well-versed in both its theory and its practice. If his reliance on God is indeed strong, he is even better off than he ...

---

in Medieval History Presented to F. M. Powicke (Oxford, 1948), 151.

12 In the *Sefer ha-Kuzari* III, 23 and 53. Under "pneumatists," the author Judah Halevi understands the magicians who sought to pull down the *pneuma* of the stars and wrote instructions on how to do so. An entire literature is dedicated to the subject of pneumatist science, e.g., the *Sefer ha-Tamar*, which I published in Hebrew (Jerusalem, 1926) and later translated into German (Hanover, 1927). The Arabic original has not survived. To this day, the book remains one of the most enigmatic texts of occult Arab literature; cf. S. Pines, "Le Sefer ha-Tamar et les Miggidim des Kabbalistes," in *Hommage à Georges Vajda* (Louvain, 1980), 333–69.

13 See Albo in the *Sefer ha-Ikkarim* 1, 8. In North Africa, around the same time (beginning of the fifteenth century), Simeon ben Ẓemaḥ Duran, who had an interest in science, polemicized against the efforts of the alchemists in his great philosophical work. Cf. his *Magen Avot* (Livorno, 1785).

The master of alchemy needs certain conditions, in whose absence he can accomplish nothing, conditions not to be found in every time and place, but the man who relies on God is assured of his livelihood in any circumstance in this world, as it is said (Deut. 8:3): "Man doth not live by bread only, but by everything that proceedeth out of the mouth of the Lord doth man live."

The master of alchemy never divulges his secret to another, fearing for himself, while the man who trusts in God does not fear anybody. Rather he boasts of his reliance, as said the sage (Ps. 56:12): "In God do I trust, I will not be afraid; what can man do unto me?" [14]

Paquda goes on to compare the alchemists' hardships and sorrows with the balanced peace of mind of those who trust in God. The author knows nothing about any damnability of the alchemical enterprise.

Even more remarkable is the derivation of the word *kimiya* (chemistry) from the Hebrew, which carried over from Arabic sources. Steinschneider cites Al-Ṣafadī; E. Wiedemann, who did not know Steinschneider's reference, quotes from Al-Sakhāwī, a fifteenth-century author. The word for chemistry comes from *ki miya* (for it is of God),[15] an etymology undoubtedly derived

---

14 Baḥya ibn Paquda, *The Book of Direction to the Duties of the Heart*, trans. M. Mansoor (Oxford and Portland, Ore. 2004), 223–24. Around 1300, in his homilies on the Pentateuch, *Derashot al ha-Torah* (Cracow, 1573), fol. 14d, Joshua ibn Shuʻaib quotes a different version of Paquda's text, which repeats the words of a Hasid that "confidence in [or devotion to] God is the true alchemy." Since I could not find the source for this quote, I assume it was either simplified or remembered inaccurately.

15 M. Steinschneider in *Jeschurun* 9 (1878): 84; E. Wiedemann, "Zur Alchemie bei den Arabern," *Journal für praktische Chemie* 76 (1907): 113. Wiedemann undoubtedly misunderstood the derivation and, as a result of his misreading, translated it as "for it is more benevolent than

from the Jews. The first Jewish alchemist can be found with certainty in Egypt in the tenth century,[16] while alchemical writings attributed to Jewish authors in the Middle Ages are based either on errors or pseudepigraphy. The Jewish alchemical work of Zadith ben Hamuel, which is mentioned by M. Bertholet, was actually written by the Islamic author Abu Abdallah Muhammad Ibn Umail al Tamimi (al-Sadik).[17] In the Hebraic literature, a treatise on alchemy was passed off as being authored by Moses Maimonides in his role as physician and naturalist. It survived in different versions in several Hebrew manuscripts as *Iggeret ha-Sodot,* in the form of epistles addressed to his famous pupil Joseph ibn Aknin. This treatise also exists in Latin translation, supposedly from the thirteenth century.[18]

When Nicholas Flamel – one of the few who, according to the mystics and alchemists, was supposed to have discovered the Philosopher's Stone – bought a papyrus[19] book in Paris, reputedly "at a small price," it was a baptized Jewish physician, not a kabbalist, who in 1378, in the pilgrimage town of Santiago de Compostela, disclosed to him the meaning of the writing and therewith the secret of alchemy. The manuscript

---

God." Steinschneider did not recognize the meaning of the etymology either.

16 This can be found in a response by Shemariah ben Elḥanan of Al-Qayrawan (Kairouan); cf. S. Assaf, *Responsa Geonica* (Jerusalem, 1942, Hebr.), 115.

17 Cf. M. Berthelot, *La Chimie au moyen âge* (Paris, 1893), vol. 1, 249, and the correction in *Orientalische Literatur-Zeitung* (1928), col. 665.

18 Cf. M. Steinschneider, *Zur pseudoepigraphischen Literatur* (Berlin, 1862), 26–27, and *Die Hebräischen Übersetzungen,* op. cit., 765 and 922. There may be a more elaborate version of this text, the ending of which is not clear, in a Hebrew manuscript at the Bodleiana Library in Oxford (Neubauer-Cowley 2, 194, no. 2779). Also included there is a recipe for the making of the Philosopher's Stone (fol. 20a).

19 On the Latin *cortex* in the sense of papyrus, see R. Eisler, in *Monatsschrift für Geschichte und Wissenschaft des Judentums* 70 (1926), 194, who believes the story, and my response, 202.

was said to have been composed by "Abraham the Jew" as instruction for his consociates. The heading supposedly read: ABRAHAM THE JEW, PRINCE, PRIEST, LEVITE, ASTROLOGER AND PHILOSOPHER, TO THE NATION OF THE JEWES BY THE WRATH OF GOD DISPERSED AMONG THE GAULES SENDETH HEALTH.[20] This heading alone proves the fictitious character of the attribution.

In any case, this account is typical of those who, in the eyes of the medieval alchemists, were the bearers of their wisdom among Jews. The existence of Hebrew translations of two writings by an author who called himself Abu Aflaḥ al-Sarakusti, but may have been fictitious, testifies to the fact that even before the spread of Kabbalah, alchemical writings were as popular in Jewish circles as other Hermetic books of Arabic literature. The surname "al-Sarakusti" points either to Syracuse in Sicily or Saragossa in Spain. If the author was indeed a physician at the court of the King of Saragossa,[21] as he claimed, then he must have been active prior to Saragossa's conquest by the Almovarids in the year 1110. The two books that survived under his name exist only in Hebrew; however, there can be no doubt that they are of Arabic origin. The author writes demonstratively as a Muslim. The first book, *Sefer ha-Tamar*, is a rather odd treatise on the theory and practice of "Pneumatist philosophy," that is, the science of capturing the pneuma of the stars by occult means. The second book, *Emek ha-Melekh*, deals with alchemy, its title, according to the author, a reference to the Philosopher's Stone. Both books are undoubtedly by the same translator, as their style is identical. Judging from the French terminology of the alchemical book, the translations originated in Provence. The general, introductory part

---

20 Eugenius Philalethes, *Magia Adamica* (London, 1650), reprinted in Thomas Vaughan, *Magical Writings,* ed. A.E. Waite (London, 1888), 113, where the story is recounted at length.

21 See C.A. Nallino, "Abu Aflaḥ arabo siracusano o saragozzano?" *Rivista dei studii orientali* 13 (1931–32), 165–71.

of the book, which remained intact,[22] corresponds, for the most part literally, to its counterpart in the *Sefer ha-Tamar*, except that in the former, the science discussed is not the doctrine of Pneumatist "workings" and effects but rather of alchemy. The second part contains detailed alchemical recipes of a chemical nature. There are no indications that Latin alchemical texts were known in Jewish circles before the end of the thirteenth century. One can safely assume that until then alchemical traditions came exclusively from Arabic sources. Judah ben Solomon ha-Kohen Matka from Toledo, who in the mid-nineteenth century authored a Hebrew encyclopedia of all sciences (which contains highly derogatory remarks about the "great art" of alchemy), was fluent in Arabic, which in his time was not only spoken by the Jews of Toledo but often used by them in their literature.[23]

Having made these preparatory remarks on the spread of alchemy among Jews, we can now return to the original question of how Kabbalah as a system of mystic symbolism relates to alchemy. The answer is one for which we would search in vain among the historians of alchemy.

The core of all alchemy, however understood, is the transmutation of base metals into gold, the highest and most noble metallic element. As a symbol of the highest moral and spiritual status, gold is the center, or goal, of the "Work" for all alchemists, including the mystics among them. Without this

---

22 Now in the British Museum, MS Gaster 19, fols. 3–22, is complete. About half is also included in MS Or. 3659 (Margoliouth 1104) in the British Museum, as well as several excerpts in the collectanea of Johanan Alemanno (MS Oxford, Cowley 2234). I published excerpts from this book in the Hebrew edition of the *Sefer ha-Tamar* (39–50).

23 The author complains that one finds poorer habits and more deceit among scholars than among fools, for some use their wisdom for make-believe or for the fabrication of gold, "which they call the 'great art' but will never bring off because it is impossible." Cf. Steinschneider, *Jeschurun* 9 (1878): 85.

premise there is no alchemy; however, the status of gold is difficult to reconcile with kabbalist symbolism. In the Kabbalah, gold is not at all a symbol of the highest status. The hundreds and hundreds of texts and lists of symbols (the latter occurring hundredfold especially in manuscripts[24]) that make up Kabbalist literature are unanimous herein (with only a few very specific exceptions): silver is the symbol of the right side, male donation, grace, and love (white, milk); in contrast, gold, the symbol of the left side, represents the female and strict Judgment (red, blood, wine).[25] This division first appears in the oldest extant kabbalist text, the *Sefer ha-Bahir*.[26] From the outset, this symbolism, conspicuous in the history of religion, does not allow for the possibility that the creation of gold would be considered essential, not according to the real, commonly shared kabbalist world scheme and surely not according to the internal, spiritual, theosophical world view. To this end, particular reinterpretations and artifices were required. How else could a kabbalist consider gold to be the highest purpose, since it represents precisely that which he still needed to *overcome* on the mystical inward path, namely, the *din,* the strict Judgment. According to Zosimos, whose alchemy leans heavily toward mysticism, the man of silver (ʼαργυσάνδρωπος)

---

24 In *Kirjath Sepher* 10 (1934), 498–515, I listed a bibliography of such "nomenclatures of the *sefirot,*" as Steinschneider calls them in his writings.

25 The first Hebrew author to point out the contradiction between the kabbalists and those "knowledgeable in nature" in regard to the valuation of gold and silver was Jacob Emden (1697–1776), a "rationalist" kabbalist, in the article on *zahab* (gold), in his lexicon of kabbalist symbols, *Ziẓim u-Feraḥim* (Altona, 1768). This is mentioned in S. Rubin, *Heidentum und Kabbala* (Vienna, 1893), 89.

26 I am quoting this in accordance with the order in my German translation of the book (Leipzig, 1923; reprinted Darmstadt, 1970). I discuss the *Bahir* at length in chapter two of my *Origins of the Kabbalah* (Princeton, 1990).

precedes the man of gold (χρυσάνδρωπος).[27] In kabbalist symbolism it would be the opposite. Therefore an antagonism arises between fundamental motifs, although the mystical alchemists would not have noticed this in their efforts to consolidate all symbolisms at any cost, especially since only a few of them would have read or been able to read authentic kabbalist texts. As mentioned before, kabbalist symbolism is rather peculiar. Elsewhere within the symbolisms of the Hellenistic-occidental world, and particularly in alchemy itself, the masculine is considered red and the feminine white, as in the naming of certain alchemical substances "white woman" and "red man." Then again, the inner Jewish, Haggadic development, which led to such paradoxical mystic concepts as the feminine as a correlative to the strict Judgment, is easily overlooked; however, this need not concern us here.

Thus it is understandable that within Judaism practical alchemy was only rarely pursued in kabbalist circles. These two areas did not fit well together and, as we will see, were connected relatively late. I have not been able to find alchemical recipes relating to the Great Work in any Hebraic kabbalist book or manuscript before 1500. Those recipes found in older manuscripts (from the fourteenth or fifteenth century) have nothing to do with Kabbalah and did not originate in Jewish tradition.[28]

Although the fundamentals of theoretical kabbalist mysticism conflict with the basic tendencies of alchemical symbolism, certain alchemical characteristics nevertheless became intermingled with the plenitude of kabbalist motifs and symbols. Here a certain influence of alchemy can be accounted for after all. Of course, it is precisely the cosmological-alchemical

---

27 Cf. Lippmann, op. cit., 81.

28 Such pieces can be found, for example, in MSS Vatican Hebr. 375, fols. 53–55 (of Italian provenance), and Munich, Hebr. 214, fol. 33b (of Spanish provenance).

symbolism of metals (and other substances that may belong in this group) that received no attention by the alchemists of the sixteenth through the nineteenth centuries and played no role whatsoever in the "Christian Kabbalah" and in Rosicrucianism. They were not, however, without significance for the knowledge of the channels through which the late-Hellenistic world affected the Jewish mysticism of the Middle Ages.

One ancient fragment that preserved the alchemical symbolism of gold as masculinity can be found in the *Bahir* (sec. 36). It did not play a role in the systematical evolution of the Kabbalah. The fragment, about which the kabbalists would have been completely ignorant after about 1230, is placed between two antipodal classical pieces of kabbalist symbolism (sections 35 and 38). It reads:

> Why is gold called זהב (*zahab*)? Because there are three principles contained in it: the masculine, *zakhar,* and the ז (*zayin*) points to that; the soul, and the ה (*he*), points to that [obviously the feminine, since the consonant *he* in the mysticism of the alphabet has always been interpreted as such]; ... and ב (*bet*) avouches its duration, as is written [in the Torah, which starts with this letter]: "in the beginning."

Here gold fulfills all the requirements of alchemical symbolism: it represents the mystical communion of the highest principles operating in the cosmos, which come about through the medium of creation – as much God's creation of the cosmos as the alchemical completion of the Work. The symbolism of the "king's daughter," which describes the function of the *bet* in the parable, corresponds – be it consciously or unconsciously – to the symbolism of the *prima materia* with the alchemists, which itself corresponds to the primal matter, the chaos during God's creation of the world. This passage, which is directed specifically toward alchemy, is rare in classical kabbalist literature. But as early as the *Tiqqunei ha-Zohar,* which uses the *Bahir* fragment (in no. 21), this is replaced by a less fitting, unexceptional interpretation (based on the number seven, that is, the seven days of Creation), since the reading of the *zayin* as a masculine principle was unacceptable to the Kabbalah. Although disjointed, this interpretation still contains a glimmer of its alchemical origin: gold as a symbol of the highest perfection of the Creation, imbued with light – evidently primal light.

The conflict between the mystical and the profane appreciation of gold in the Kabbalah is sharply expressed by the attempts of the kabbalists to explain why the value relationship between gold and silver in the natural, lower world is the reverse of that in the spiritual, upper world. These attempts at explanation spread from one classical passage in the *Sefer ha-Zohar* – the main text of Spanish Kabbalah, authored between 1280 and 1285 – to many other works. Since the status of gold could at least be maintained in the lower Merkabah (*merkavah*, divine chariot) and its contingent sensible world, there would have been room for purely material, alchemical efforts, but this put an end even more strongly to the spiritual reinterpretation of alchemy as a mystical practice.

The above-mentioned passage in the *Zohar* (2:197*b*) reads:

> Come and see, here [in Exodus 35:5] gold is listed first and silver second because it corresponds to the lower enumeration method [perhaps: from the lower world?]. Had he [Moses] wanted to count according to the enumeration method of the upper Merkabah, he would have begun counting on the right [e.g., from the silver] and only then on the left. Why? Because it is written [Haggai 2:8]: "Silver is Mine and gold is Mine – silver first and gold afterwards.[29] But in the

---

29 This is the order in the world of the divine *sefirot,* which is the upper world. Haggai 2:8 is also the key verse in the *Bahir* for the symbolism of gold and silver. In the Hebrew MS Hamburg 252 (Steinschneider 24), fol. 23*b,* this verse concludes a Spanish Jewish alchemical recipe.

lower Merkabah one begins on the left and only then [continues] on the right side, as it is written [Exodus 35:5]: "Gold, silver, and copper."

The passage is clear, and the reversed order of the upper and lower worlds is a motif frequently used in the older Kabbalah. It played into the later theory of many kabbalists that the creation of the lower world came about by mirroring the "reflected light" of the world of the *sefirot.* Thus one finds this motif in the Talmudic sequence of the letters of the alphabet in both worlds and thenceforth in the theory of the mystical names of God and the *Ephesia Grammata* (Ephesian Letters). To this line of thought also belongs the attribution in the book *Esh Meẓaref* (which will be discussed below) of the Philosopher's Stone to the last *sefirah* and lead (the least precious metal) to the second highest. The kabbalists may never have been cognizant of the possible Gnostic-antinomian consequences of this concept. How else, for instance, would certain texts have been allowed to be circulated that, according to this principle, not only sanctioned but commanded marriages that are forbidden by the Torah in the upper worlds?[30]

Even more radical is a passage in the pseudepigraphic *Sefer ha-Peli'ah,*[31] written around 1400, which follows the same fundamental idea. With clear examples from everyday life, it explains that gold is more valued in our world because we live in the eon of Gold, under the power of the strict Judgment. The passage shifts the mystically correct valuation to the eon of Mercy, which preceded the eon of Gold that was ruled by the *sefirah* Ḥesed.[32] Expositions of this kind are clearly in opposition to alchemical thinking.

---

30 See the *Sefer ha-Temunah* on the letter ש (*shin*) (Lemberg, 1892), fols. *22a-b* and *62a-b*: "What is forbidden in the one, is permitted in the other."

31 *Sefer ha-Peli'ah* (Korets, 1784), fol. *16c.*

32 A different attempt to explain the higher valuation of gold can

It is unclear whether *Zohar* 1:249b–250a is influenced by alchemy. It states that "were it not for the ferocious beasts breeding [in the gold-dust covered mountains], human beings would not be poor, because the power of the sun proliferates gold."[33] Then again it was precisely the opponents of alchemy who drew from this "natural" relationship of the sun to gold an argument against the possibility of artificial transmutation of metals. Hence Judah ben Salomon ha-Kohen Matka of Toledo says: "The scholars think that gold evolves in nature over long time periods while alchemy believes it can accomplish this in the short term."[34] *Zohar* 2:172a describes this influence somewhat differently. Inspired by astrology and alchemy, it discusses the influence of the stars on the "growth" of metals, wherefore the author invokes a (fictitious?) book by King Solomon "on the science of precious metals," which probably relates to one of the many lapidaries that were widespread in the Middle Ages. Prior to that he cites a related belief from an alleged "book of higher Oriental sciences," which

---

be found in Naphtali ben Jacob Elhanan Bacharach's *Emek ha-Melekh* (Amsterdam, 1648, fols. 28d–29a), according to which silver is so subtle as to be spiritually accessible only to few, with most seeking the harder, cruder gold. Another explanation is given by Shneur Zalman of Lyady, one of the leaders of the Ḥabad-Ḥasidim: silver is only a single Mercy, while gold represents an abundance of Mercy and thus ranks higher than silver.

33 Cf. *Zohar* 2:236b. That metals would "grow" like plants corresponds not only to Alexandrian ideas (e.g., in Silberer, op. cit., 75) but also to theories like those of the Arabic alchemist of the twelfth century whose writings were translated into Latin under the name of Artephius. According to him, plants grow in water or earth while metals originate from sulphur and quicksilver. The heat of the sun permeates the earth and combines with these elements to form gold (*Encyclopedia Judaica*, vol. 2, col. 544). The assertion made there (col. 547) that Artephius was a baptized Jew, not an Arab, is probably not correct. On Artephius, cf. also Waite, *The Secret Tradition of Alchemy* (London, 1926), 111–12.

34 Cf. *Jeschurun* 9: 85.

deals with magical remedies and precious metals. According to that book, a particularly prized type of gold grows on high mountains, where water is scarce, under the influence of comets rather than ordinary stars.[35]

A passage strongly influenced by alchemy is found in *Zohar* 2:23b–24b. While there are no literal alchemical statements found there, it does offer a complete system of alchemical symbolism. Two word-for-word counterparts can be found in the Hebrew writings of Moses de Leon, who is regarded as the main author of the *Zohar*.[36] A close comparison shows that precedence should be given here to the pseudo-Aramaic *Zohar*, which was, in part, copied and, in part, paraphrased and explicated by the author in his later Hebrew writings. Based on the Aristotelian model of the relation of the four elements to the four qualities (warm, cold, dry, humid),[37] the following correspondence of the elements to metals and directionals is

---

35 Also curious is the passage in *Zohar* 2:188a, where it says, in connection with news about the pagan sun-worship that these worshippers, through ancient traditions, possess knowledge from the sun that allows them to spot gold and silver. This is described in more detail there.

36 Both passages are in *Sheqel ha-Kodesh* (London, 1911), 118–22, and in the long fragment of a yet to be identified text by Moses de Leon, in MS Munich Hebr. 47, fols. 366ff. and 386ff.; cf. my essay in *Monatsschrift für Geschichte und Wissenschaft des Judentums* (1927), 109–23. The alchemical character of this passage was mentioned by R. Eisler, *Weltmantel und Himmelszelt* (Munich, 1910), vol. 2, 452; and before him by I. Stern, in *Ben-Chananja* III (1860), 178, according to whom, "in the metals there is a gleam of alchemy."

37 This model was developed by Aristotle (in *De generatione et corruptione* II, 1–3), who expressly states that these four qualities affect the formation of metals. This was pointed out by A. Jellinek in *Beiträge zur Geschichte der Kabbala* (Leipzig, 1852), 38. The author of the *Zohar* would not necessarily have drawn on the translation of Aristotle by Moses ibn Tibbon, finished in 1250; he may just as easily have used a medieval source of which there were many that repeated this particular Aristotelian notion.

developed there (for which I could not find an exact parallel, having only inadequate knowledge of the later or earlier alchemical literature [38]):

"upper Merkabah" *primary metals*	Fire	Water	Air	Earth
	North	South	East	West
	Gold	Silver	Copper	Iron

"lower Merkabah" *secondary metals*	Brass	Lead	Tin [39]	Iron (Steel?)

The secondary metals are supposed to originate from the primary ones by combining their element with Earth. The *Zohar* passage presents a long rigmarole of transmutations and interrelations that are strikingly formulaic. In the two parallel

---

38 Neither Lippmann nor Ruska mentions anything of that kind in their works. The kabbalist correspondence of gold to the North is otherwise alien to alchemical symbolism and is derived from Job 37:22: "By the north wind the golden rays emerge."

39 The old Talmudic-Greek word *kassitra* (κασσίτερος). The *Zohar* adds the following explanation: "which is a lower [literally, smaller] copper." Likewise, Moses de Leon writes, without mentioning the old word at all, only *neḥoshet takhton* (op. cit., 122): "a lower form of copper." About brass he writes (op. cit.): "yellow copper, metal of earth." The first of these synonyms comes from Ezra 8:27. The name is universally used for brass, also in the Middle Ages; cf. Lippmann, op. cit., 571ff. The *Zohar* defines this metal as yellow dross, which looks like gold. The translation of this passage in J. de Pauly, *Sepher-ha-Zohar: Le livre de la splendeur* (Paris, 1908), vol. 3, 121, is full of errors. His remark in vol. 4, 279, where he finds in this alchemical cosmology the "Holy Trinity," sheds sufficient light on the quality of his translation. Just as brass is the dross of gold, so elsewhere lead is called a scoria of silver (in the continuation of the *Zohar* passage on physiognomy, printed in the *Zohar Ḥadash,* fol. 33d). Here Adam's mystical transformation into Abraham is described, whereby silver "produces scoria, which emerges outward as lead." This is repeated in the review of physiognomy in the *Tiqqunei ha-Zohar,* no. 70, fol. 128b. And the *Raaya Meheimna,* written by the same author as the *Tiqqunim,* knows of lead as "dirt" or scoria during the smelting of silver.

texts, Moses de Leon also draws on the biblical symbolism of the four streams of Paradise and the twelve oxen of the Brazen Sea in the Temple of Solomon. I should mention that the specific passage in the printed text by Leon (as well as in the handwritten copies I consulted) is slightly corrupted but can be reconstructed. Here one finds an explicit reference to alchemists: "Copper is red and brings about the nature of both [gold and silver] because those *who know the Work* make from it gold and silver."[40] The denotation for alchemists, ποιηταί

---

40 The Hebrew term here is *ha-yodim ba-melakhah*. In the Hebrew translation of the *Emek ha-Melekh*, the alchemists are also called *ba'alei melakhah* (artisans). Without naming his source, D. Chwolson in *Die Ssabier und der Ssabismus* (St. Petersburg, 1856), p. 660, mentions this expression, next to *ba'alei omanut* (artists), as a technical term used by Spanish Jews for alchemists. A single detail of the alchemical work is called *pe'ulah* (act); the Great Work, however, is called *melakhah* (craft), so that, for instance, at the beginning of the *Emek ha-Melekh*, "the execution of the Great Work" is rendered in Hebrew as *pe'ulah ha melakhah*. The term *melakhah*, in this particular sense, is familiar in the sixteenth century, cf. Moses Cordovero's *Pardes Rimmonim* (Cracow, 1592), fol. 72b, and Simeon Labi's *Zohar* commentary, *Ketem Paz* (Livorno, 1795), fol. 445a. For a long time I considered the well-known work of magic, *Des Juden Abraham von Worms Buch der wahren Praktik in der uralten göttlichen Magie* – translated into both German and English (via French) allegedly from a Hebrew manuscript of 1387 and supposedly published in Cologne in 1725 (more likely in 1800) – to be of Jewish origin; cf. *Monatsschrift für Geschichte und Wissenschaft des Judentums* 69, p. 95, and *Bibliographia Kabbalistica* (1927), p. 2. I changed my mind when I found clear evidence of the writings of Pico della Mirandola and his juxtaposition of Kabbalah and magic not only in the title but in the text of the book itself. The book was, in fact, written in the sixteenth century by a non-Jew who possessed a striking knowledge of Hebrew. This author also uses the term *melakhah* for alchemy (IV, 7), but only in the German translation! It is the same book that found wide distribution in occult circles in its English version as *The Book of Secret Magic by Abra-Melin the Mage, as Delivered by Abraham the Jew unto his Son Lamech, A.D. 1458*, trans. S.L. Mathers (London, 1898). Mathers

(Latin, *artistæ*), is a standing formula transcribed here into Hebrew for the "work" in the sense of the Great Work of alchemy, which in the Hebrew literature has been used for centuries.[41] Although neither Moses de Leon nor the above-mentioned *Zohar* passage expressly refers to the *sefirot*, there can be little doubt that the four elements and the four primary metals correspond to the four *sefirot: Ḥesed, Gevurah, Tif'eret,* and *Malkhut.* Thus *Tif'eret* represents copper, the union of gold and silver; and *Malkhut*, iron. If the mystical ascension were to proceed from the lowest *sefirah* or from the purification of metals, then the lowest *sefirah* would correspond to the *prima materia,* with which the alchemical Work begins. Copper would then be a preliminary phase, from which gold and silver, both united within it, are produced. This corresponds to the interpretation of copper in a *Zohar* passage (2:138b) that discusses the materials listed in Exodus 25:3 (gold, silver, and copper) that are needed for the construction of the Tabernacle. There it says that the (primarily reddish) copper unites in itself the colors, as well as the qualities, of gold and silver, whereby those of gold dominate. This is consistent with the above-cited passage by Moses de Leon, which refers specifically to the alchemists.[42] Indeed, it is well established that many alchemists regarded copper as a preliminary stage of silver and gold, just as Zosimos, in his much cited alchemical-mystical vision, knew of three stages: the copper homunculus, the man of silver, and the man of gold (Lippmann, op. cit., 80). The post-*Zohar* generation occasionally uses the above passage (2:23b) as is, but often there are other associations of the metals with the sky directionals and

---

was not aware of the German original – which is preserved in many manuscripts – parts of which date back to the sixteenth century.

41 This linguistic usage was familiar to the seventeenth-century author of the *Esh Meẓaref.*

42 Waite's interpretation in his *The Secret Tradition in Alchemy,* 390, as the *sefirot Netsah* and *Hod* is, like most of the book, wrong.

the *sefirot,* which are based on a system completely different from that of the *Zohar.*[43]

The color symbolism of gold is divided into yellow and red. In the *Zohar* passage discussed above (2:171*b*), yellow appears as the color of gold, as it does in Moses de Leon's *Sheqel ha-Kodesh,* which says (120):

> Gold comes into being from and is connected with the mystery of fire and the North, because when natural warmth approaches that which is cold, it produces a yellow nature, and that is the mystery of gold ... Silver is attached to the mystery of water and the South, because when water is combined with the sun, it produces a white nature, which is the mystery of silver. But copper is red and brings about the nature of both [gold and silver], because those who know about the Work are able to make from it the nature of silver and gold.

In other respects, red is always the color of gold. The symbolism of gold, as it is found in several places in the *Zohar,* is based primarily on a passage from the Babylonian Talmud *(Yoma* 44*b*), which has several parallels in the Midrashim, where seven types of biblical gold are listed.[44]

---

43 Writing in Spain around 1500, the kabbalist Joseph of Ḥamadan from Persia used this *Zohar* passage in his work on the Tabernacle, MS British Museum (Margoliouth 464), fol. 31*b*, and connected it to the eight vestments of the high priest. The eight metals originate from the eight vestments of God, which correspond to those of the high priest. However, the author counts only seven metals, as in the *Zohar,* whereby he uses periphrases for brass and tin such as "another [lower?] kind of gold" (see n. 39) and "polished copper" (this is from 2 Chron. 4:16). Other models of the correspondence between the metals and the directionals are given by Isaac ben Samuel of Acre, *Me'irat Enayim,* MS Munich Hebr. 17, fol. 27*b*. Another variant is by the anonymous author of *Ma'arekhet ha-Elohut* (Mantua, 1558), fol. 223*a*.

44 Similar in the Midrash on the Song of Songs 3:17 and in *Ba-Midbar rabba,* sec. 12.

Incidentally, the above-mentioned Talmud passage reflects a knowledge of the change in color from yellow to red. For instance, the seven types of gold were interpreted mystically by some kabbalists, undoubtedly in the spirit of the alchemists, as the complex of the seven lower *sefirot*. There is a curious passage in *Zohar* 2:73a, which belongs to a section titled *Raza de-Razin* that deals with physiognomy and evidently is related to the medieval *Secretum Secretorum*, a widely circulated pseudo-Aristotelian tractate on politics, which also discusses physiognomy.[45] Here the symbolism of the seven types of gold is used in the description of David's face:

> In the book of Adam[46] I have seen written the following: the shapes [of the face] of the first redeemer[47] resembles the moon. His face was greenish gold; his beard, gold from Ophir; his eyebrows, Sheba's gold; his eyelashes, gold from Parvaim; his hair, Sagur (solid or "locked") gold;[48] his chest, refined gold;[49] both his arms, gold from Tarshish.

----

45 Cf. Steinschneider, *Hebräische Übersetzungen,* 245–59, and M. Gaster, *Studies and Texts* (London, 1925), vol. 2, 742–813.

46 In the *Zohar,* the twenty references to such a book of Adam have no uniform character. It is not clear whether this particular passage corresponds to a real quotation. Most of the quotations are unabashedly fictitious, especially those dealing with the kabbalist prayer mysticism.

47 The first redeemer or Messiah is generally understood to be Moses, while the reference to David alludes to kabbalist symbolism. The relation of David to the moon belongs to the ironclad foundation of kabbalist symbolism and has entered its trove of symbols in the form of the last *sefirah Malkhut,* called the "kingdom" (of David or God).

48 For the most part, these types of gold are named in the Bible after their geographical place of origin. "Locked gold" derives from 1 Kings 6:20, where it actually means pressed or flattened gold. The Talmud interprets it as follows: when this gold is being sold, all other stores are locked (closed). See also note 59.

49 This type of gold is mentioned in 1 Kings 10:18 as a component in the throne of Solomon.

This passage, which lets David's face radiate in all seven types of gold (despite the fact that the moon alchemically relates to silver), seems to be rather conspicuous and remarkable in its obscurity. It is not surprising that David's reddish hair, which is described in the Book of Samuel, would evoke the symbolism of gold. Curiously, this symbolism of gold in relation to the moon is mentioned nowhere else except in this passage. In the *Tiqqunim,* written shortly after the composition of the main part of the *Zohar,* the seven types of gold are also related to hair.[50] The *Zohar* still speaks of David's eyes as having been composed of the full color spectrum and their beauty having been such that no other like it existed in the world.

Two related but diametrically opposed interpretations can be found back to back in the *Zohar:* the first ranks the seven types of gold below silver, according to the classical schema; the other, however, reads like a mystical meditation using alchemical terminology, as if the author wanted a familiar interpretation to be followed by a more profound one. This sequence in the otherwise uniform *Zohar* passage can only be understood in this way. Paradoxically, the second interpretation functions as a continuation of the first, even though it invalidates it. The commentators of the *Zohar* made great efforts to reinterpret this passage in terms of the Kabbalah. Baron Christian Knorr von Rosenroth cites it in his *Kabbala Denudata* (1:298), without calling attention to any relationship with alchemy. Devoid of any explanation, his translation is incomprehensible and partially incorrect. (The short paraphrasing of the passage in de Pauly's French translation is practically useless.) In the following, as always, my additions are enclosed in brackets:

> Why, it says there are seven types of gold. And if you
> mean that gold, after all, is strength and silver is love,

---

50 *Tiqqunim,* no. 17, fol. 123*b.*

how can gold be ranked above it [silver]?[51] – it is not so. Because gold is indeed higher than any other, [not the common, natural gold] but in the mystical way,[52] and that is the "higher, mystical gold," which is the seventh of those [seven] types of gold. And it is a gold that shines and glints in the eyes. And such is [this gold] that, when it appears in the world, whoever obtains it hides it inside himself, and from there [e.g., from this mystical gold] all other types of gold emanate. And when is gold [rightly] called gold?[53] When it shines and ascends to the glory [of the mystical region] of the "fear of God,"[54] and then it is in [the state of] the "mystical bliss," which can provide joy also for the lower [regions]. And when it is in the state of "strictness," [that is,] when it passes from that color[55]

---

51 The original text is quite corrupted. I read *we-'ist'laq* as a question, as if it were written *we-'eikh 'ist'laq;* but perhaps it should simply be read as silver instead of gold. Then it would translate into "and silver is ranked above gold."

52 A very popular expression in the *Zohar, be'orakh stim* indicates the internalization of a concept.

53 The color-mystical meditation that follows describes different states of the mystical gold in the soul. The fact that it became a headache for *Zohar* commentators is indirect proof of the fact that the mystical reinterpretation and application of alchemical symbols, which is manifest here unambiguously, was alien to these later authors, particularly those of the sixteenth and seventeenth centuries. There is a related homily on gold and silver in the *Sha'ar ha-Razim,* written between 1280 and 1290 in Toledo by Todros ben Joseph ha-Levi Abulafia (MS Munich Hebr. 209, fol. 53*b*), wherein gold corresponds to the higher *sefirah Binah,* perhaps even to Ḥokhma, the uppermost *sefirah.* This book uses parts of the *Zohar.*

54 Fear and love are the uppermost states of the soul in their relationship to God, whereby the kabbalists relate this uppermost fear of God to the *sefirah Binah,* which stands above Ḥesed, the *sefirah* of love. In the printed Hebrew texts the genitive preposition "of" is omitted.

55 *Gavan* (color) may be understood here, as it often is in the *Zohar,* in the sense of essence, state, or quality. Its meaning is: the gold that

into blue, black, and red, then it is the [gold in the region of] "stern strictness." But the [true] gold belongs to joy and has its place where the fear of god ascends and joy soars.[56] Silver is among it, [according to] the mystery of the right arm, because the highest [mystical] head is "of gold," as it is written [in Daniel 2:38]: "You are the head of gold." "Its breast and arms were of silver" [ibid., 2:32] points to the lower [region]. But when the "silver" becomes perfected, it is contained in "gold." And this is the secret [of Proverbs 25:11]: "Like golden apples in silver showpieces." Thus it unfolds that [in the true perfection] silver becomes gold,[57] and then its place is perfect. And therefore there are seven types of gold.[58] And copper comes

---

corresponds to the stage of Rigor – the classical symbolism of the Kabbalah – is not at all the uppermost, mystical gold, which corresponds to the highest stage attainable through meditation, which is that of the "fear of God." This explication of the rank of true gold versus silver derives from the fact that in the Spanish Kabbalah of the *Zohar* and in the writings of Moses de Leon this uppermost stage was reassigned to the *sefirah Binah,* which cannot be surpassed though meditation (in the Hebrew of Moses de Leon *hitbonenut,* contemplation); while love was moved to the next *sefirah, Ḥesed.*

56 Here the notion of the *simḥah shel mitzvah* – the joy that lies in the execution of the commandments – may come into play.

57 The use of the verb *ithaddar* in the sense of "to become" is very common in the *Zohar* and accords with medieval linguistic usage.

58 The "therefore" is only explained by what comes next. Its meaning is: man is made up of seven main parts (cf. in the *Bahir,* pars. 55, 114, and 116, and also often in the *Zohar*), which correspond to the seven *sefirot,* from *Binah* to *Yesod* – here, as in the following left-out lines, we have byssus as the color symbol of *Yesod* – or to the seven stages that man can traverse in his meditations. In their original, harmonized state, in the body of the primordial man or *macroanthropos,* all are gold – albeit of, more or less, little value. Those who systematically restore in themselves the original form of man transform their soul into gold – represented in the respective regions by "copper," "silver," etc. – if they advance on the uppermost stage, the head, i.e., the region of the *Binah,* called above "fear of God." Only

[also] out of gold, when it is changed towards the
bad, and this is the left arm. The left thigh is blue; the
right thigh is purple and it is contained in the left one
… But the "higher [mystical] gold" is a hidden secret
and his name is "locked gold" [1 Kings 6:20],[59] concealed and hidden from all, and therefore it is called
solid, because it is kept from the eye so that it has no
power over it [e.g., cannot perceive it]; the "lower"
gold, however, is somewhat more perceptible.[60]

Not even Christian and Gnostic mystics and alchemists
could have described the "gold" within the human soul more
clearly than this characteristic piece of kabbalist theosophy.
This is the only passage in the *Zohar* that uses the transmutation of silver to gold for mystical interpretations *expressis ver-
bis,* that is, presupposes it as a fact in the real world. Had the
tendencies toward a truly alchemical symbolism, as expressed
here and in the *Bahir* fragment mentioned above (par. 36), asserted themselves in the Kabbalah, then it would have been
justified to contend an essential relatedness between alchemy
and Kabbalah. But instead these tendencies were on the whole
eliminated from the Kabbalah. The complete opposition of this
passage to the one in *Zohar 2:197b* (discussed above) is self-ev-
ident. As a comparison with similar descriptions of what the
alchemical mystics called "philosophical gold" – in the *Zohar*

---

from there, according to mystical conception, will all parts obtain
their true place.

59 Evidently Moses de Leon had this *Zohar* passage in mind when
he wrote in the *Sheqel ha-Kodesh* (46): "They [the wise, meaning those
of the *Zohar* whose teachings Leon sought to propagate in his Hebrew
writings already as ancient Mishnaic wisdom] say that the most valuable among all types of gold is the locked gold because it is a gold that
is kept from the eye and, generally, kept from all."

60 This is not about natural metals, as is clear from this ending.
The whole passage gives a good idea of the difficulties of translating
and interpreting the intrinsically kabbalist parts of the *Zohar*.

called "mystical gold" (*zahab 'ila'a*) – here is a passage from Johann Isaac Hollandus quoted in Silberer's book (101):

> The philosophers have written much about lead ... and it is my opinion that this saturnine work should not be understood in regard to common lead but to the lead of the philosopher. Know, my child, that the stone called Philosopher's Stone comes from Saturn. And know as a truth that in the entire vegetative work [called so because of the symbolism of sowing and growing] there is no greater secret than in Saturn. Because even in [common] gold we do not find the perfection found in Saturn, since understood inwardly [pneumatically], it [Saturn] is good gold. Most philosophers agree with this, and it is only necessary for you to remove everything that is superfluous in it. Then, when you turn the inside to be the outside, which is redness, it becomes good gold ... All those strange parables, where the philosophers talked mystically about a stone, a moon, an oven, a vessel – all that is Saturn [e.g., all talk about humans]; because you must not add anything extraneous, except for what emanates from itself. None in the world is too poor to undertake and execute the Work.

The seven grades of alchemical purification – corresponding to the steps of contemplation that pervade so many mystical systems and stand for an inward process of integration – were already known by Zosimos. [61]

It cannot not be ruled out that the alchemical parlance and symbolism might eventually have encroached upon unrelated kabbalist territory. I know of two such instances, which were derived with high probability or certainty from alchemical terminology. In the *Zohar*, however, they assumed a completely different course.

---

61 Silberer, op. cit., 190; Lippmann, op. cit., 79–81.

One concerns the short mystical sentences containing what appears to be a kind of witches' multiplication table, especially in *Zohar* 1:77a (but also in 1:32b, 1:72b, 2:12b, 2:95a, and 3:162a): "One ascends to one side, one descends to the other, one enters between two. Two crown themselves in three, three enter into one." The literal sense of the sentences is often not difficult to determine and much less exciting than the pathetic formulation surmises, but it is the external form that is interesting. The sentences sound like old formulas underlaid with new, fitting meaning. Such usage of old formulas that have become incomprehensible can already be found in the *Bahir*. Strikingly similar sentences have indeed played a large role in alchemy. I already mentioned that the fictional "Maria the Jewess" appears in the oldest alchemical literature as a great authority. The following sentence is attributed to her: "Two are one, three and four are one, one will become two, two will become three."[62] This sentence, though not understood by medieval alchemists but nevertheless passed on through the centuries as alchemical mystery words,[63] can still be found in the widespread Latin versions of the (originally Arabic) *Turba Philosophorum*.[64] In one of his early books, Waite saw in the literary form of the *Turba* – a transcript of speeches by the old philosophers – a certain affinity and relation to the *Zohar*, namely, with the *Idra rabba*. In this important section, Rabbi Shim'on and his companions describe a gathering of the

---

62 Cf. J. Ruska, *Turba Philosophorum* (Berlin, 1931), 241.

63 There were many such formulas. Probably the most famous one, "Nature delights in nature, nature surpasses nature, nature conquers nature," is also cited by the kabbalist Joseph Gikatilla, a contemporary of the *Zohar*, in his commentary to the Passover Haggadah, *Perush Haggadah shel Pesaḥ* (Venice, 1602), p. 16 in the Jerusalem edition (which is attributed erroneously to Solomon ibn Adret).

64 The scholarship on the *Turba* has been completely revised by Ruska's work and the studies in M. Plessner, *Vorsokratische Philosophie und griechische Alchemie in arabisch-lateinischer Überlieferung* (Wiesbaden, 1975).

(fictional) great adepts in the Kabbalah during which speeches are given on the mystical shape of the Godhead and its secrets. But Waite was under the misapprehension that the pseudo-Aramaic word *idra* meant "assembly" or "synod," in accordance with the Latin *turba* (crowd). This meaning of the word *idra*, however, is a more recent development.[65]

The second symbolism is found in numerous places in the *Zohar*,[66] and I consider it to be incontrovertibly of alchemical origin. It deals with the demonic, the hypertrophy of the "left side of the world," the "defiled gold," "scoria of gold," or "dross of gold." Here the classical kabbalist symbolism, for which gold is the symbol of the left side, of the strict Judgment, accords to some extent with alchemy, which extracts the "philosophical gold" from the scoria and scum of metals both in nature and in the soul. The demonic, represented primarily by Samael, the prince of the Left, emerged from the hypertrophic abundance of strictness as refuse or filth.[67] One of the terms used here, *hitukhei* (literally, to smelt),[68] presupposes the notion of a smelting process wherein scoria or scum remains as waste.

---

65 Cf. A.E. Waite, *The Doctrine and Literature of the Kabbalah* (London, 1902), 460. The Zoharic linguistic usage of the word *idra* has been analyzed in depth by J. Liebes in his dissertation "Studies on the Lexicography of the Zohar" (Jerusalem, 1977, Hebr.).

66 *Zohar* 1:48*a*, 1:52*a*, 1:62*b*, 1:73*a*, 1:109*b*, 1:118*b*, 1:161*b*, 1:193*a*, 1:228*a*, 2:24*b*, 2:104*a*, 2:148*b*, 2:149*b*, 2:203*a*, 2:224*b*, 2:236*a*-*b*, 2:275*a*, 3:51*a*, 3:84*b*. See also in the *Zohar Ḥadash* on the Song of Songs (Warsaw, 1885; identical in pagination with the 1953 Jerusalem edition), 55*b*, 66*b*.

67 Thus expressly in *Zohar* 1:161*b* (*Tosefta*): "Samael who emerged from the waste of the abundant strength of Isaac." Elsewhere (1:74*b*) we read of the "waste of the strict Judgment" as the "other dominion."

68 The original meaning of *hitukhei* as smelting is still apparent in passages such as *Zohar* 2:167*b*: "The waste of metals derives from the smelting"; cf. K. Preis, "Die Medizin im Sohar," *Monatsschrift für Geschichte und Wissenschaft des Judentums* 72 (1928), 170, as well as an article on *suspita* in J. Liebes, op. cit., 336–38.

To this also belongs the terminology, long unexplained, of *suspita di-dahaba,* which is common throughout the main part of the *Zohar,* where it explicitly states that it is identical to *hitukhei.*[69] Fifty years ago, I could not explain the meaning of this term and indulged in erroneous speculation. R. Eisler's conjecture that it is derived from the Greek συσσίπτη (namely, *hyle),* meaning *putrifactio* (decay or putrefaction of matter),[70] is no longer sustainable, although at the time I agreed with him.[71] Rather, *suspita* is one of many neologisms created by Moses de Leon from Talmudic words; in this case, it is a deformation of the word *kuspa* (pomace, or husk, as in *Ta'anit* 24b).[72] The expression *zuhamah ha-zahab* was in use by the tenth century by the so-called Brothers of Purity in Basra as an alchemical term for "dregs of the metals."[73] Of course these dregs play a large role in any alchemical practice. Here, the author of the *Zohar,* who also knew Arabic, adopts a common terminology and uses it in a kabbalistic sense. These substances are varyingly called "dregs," "scoria," or "dross," words used synonymously throughout the *Zohar.*[74] *Suspita,* however, is used only in connection with gold; we do not yet know why. The word used for the "dregs" of silver, which in the *Zohar* is identified

---

69 *Zohar* 2:224b and 2:236b. It is remarkable that, except for two incomprehensible passages that seem to deal with mystical formulas (1:30a and *Tiqqunim* 132b), this word is always used in connection with gold. There is no *suspita* of gold or silver in the *Zohar.* Perhaps an explicit term for the scoria of gold existed. In 1:118b it is said sententiously: "Wherever gold is found, scoria goes unmentioned," which here is related to Isaac (Judgment) and Ismael.

70 Eisler, in *Monatsschrift für Geschichte und Wissenschaft des Judentums* 69 (1925), 365. He could not provide evidence for the Greek σύσσηψις in alchemical writings.

71 See my remark on Eisler's article, ibid., 371–72.

72 See J. Levy, *Wörterbuch über die Talmudim und Midrashim* (Berlin, 1924), vol. 2, 370.

73 This was established by Lippmann, op. cit., 379.

74 See notes 66 and 68 above.

in several places with lead (*Zohar* 3:124a; *Tiqqunim* 67; *Zohar Ḥadash* fol. 33d), is *zuhamah.*

These are the only purely alchemical traces I have been able to find in the *Zohar.* To these can be added a further parallelism that was pointed out to me by R. Alleau in Paris in 1972. It is undeniable that the symbolism of the *Shekhinah,* the female aspect of the divine world of the *sefirot* – which represents the last of the ten steps of emanation within the Godhead, as it is richly developed in the *Zohar* – exhibits close parallels to the alchemical symbolism of the *prima materia.* I addressed the kabbalist symbolism of the *Shekhinah* many years ago in the *Eranos Yearbook.*[75] Many of the symbols discussed therein reappear in the alchemical literature of the later Middle Ages, where especially the moon and the corresponding symbolism of the female are developed in connection with the *prima materia* of the alchemical Work. I do not believe that there are historical contexts for this; nevertheless, there is a structural relation between the ascension from the lowest to the highest *sefirah* and the alchemical steps involved in the refining of the philosophical gold according to a mystical view of the *ars magna.* By their very nature, the symbols available for such descriptions were limited, not to mention the fact that their source, the Old Testament, was shared equally by Jewish kabbalists and Christian alchemists. I am not sure that it is necessary to resort to the more far-reaching psychological hypothesis of archetypes of the soul, as developed by C.G. Jung in his respective works.

There are only a few connections between kabbalist and alchemical ideas in the generations following the publication of the *Zohar.* In his *Responsum* on the transmigration of souls, the fourteenth-century Toledo rabbi Judah ben Asher compared

---

75 "Zur Entwicklungsgeschichte der kabbalistischen Konzeption der Schechinah," *Eranos Yearbook* 21 (1952), 45–107, and reprinted, in revised form, in my *On the Mystical Shape of the Godhead: Basic Concepts in the Kabbalah* (New York, 1991).

the purification of souls during the process of the *Gilgul* with the corresponding alchemical process of refining metals, both of which are attained in multiple stages.[76] Perhaps further examination of kabbalist literature, especially the handwritten sources, will bring to light more connections. The most astonishing development took place at the end of the fifteenth century in Spain, in the form of revelations written down by the renowned rabbi and humanist Joseph Taitaẓak around 1480.[77] In these very curious revelations, God Himself lectures on various occult disciplines. Taitaẓak is the first kabbalist to identify alchemy with mystical theology, even before the Christian humanists pursued this line. This is even more remarkable as none of the great kabbalists of the sixteenth century (among them, students or students of students of Taitaẓak, during his activities in Salonica until about 1535) ever adopted these thoughts. Neither Joseph Caro nor Moses Cordovero knows anything about that. Parts of Taitaẓak's revelations were known in these circles, but we cannot say whether they contained any passages on alchemy. There are two passages dealing with alchemy in a handwritten manuscript in the British Museum (Margoliouth, no. 766) that contains large sections of these revelations. They also refer to a detailed instruction on the subject at hand, which no longer exists (at least not in the manuscripts known to me). Folio 107*a* reads:

> You will instantly understand the whole mystery of the lower world and the mystery of the upper and lower [mystical and worldly] silver and gold, and once you know the great science, you will instantly know how to make, in effect, without difficulty, in the lower world, each of the seven kinds of metals. And this is the science of alchemy, which is the science of

---

76 The text is included in the collection *Ṭa'am Zeḵenim* by Eliezer Ashkenazi and Raphael Kirchheim (Frankfurt, 1855), fol. 66*a*.

77 About these revelations, see my essay in *Sefunot* (Annual of the Ben-Zvi Institute), vol. 11 (1977), 67–112 (in Hebrew).

the Godhead, as you will understand when you reach it [in these revelations]. And who does not know the science of the upper world [Kabbalah] beforehand, cannot practice it [alchemy].

Mercury is named as the material to use with the seven types of metal. The next sentence in the manuscript, most of which is corrupted, assures the adept that he could put the result of his labor into the fire or under the hammer a thousand times, evidently without any harm.

> And one must perform this [the Work] in secrecy, so that no one [in the manuscript, no tree] sees it except for the one who processes it [or works with it], because this is the power [of the Work] that it would die instantly otherwise. And I [e.g., God] will tell you further below the secret [of the transmutation], and with it you will find your livelihood and live like the masters and no other art will be required than this, so that you can devote yourself to my Torah.

The continuation on folio 107b states that the *sefirah Binah* is the mystical gold of the true Kabbalah and "the secret of the smelting [or purification (*heezdak'khoot*, הזדככות) of the true kabbalist metals] is contained in the mystery of the Godhead." This authentic, mystical alchemy has a counterpart, the manuscript continues, in the alchemy of impurity known to non-Jewish scholars:

> Thus there are men among the sages of peoples with an impure soul who attained it [the mystery of the transmutation of metals], and if in the ancient days the sages of peoples with an impure soul stepped forward, it is up to you to step forward on the side of Kabbalah ... and you [the recipient of these revelations] will need the knowledge of these secrets in the time to come, when the hardships are so great that no one will be able to live [without it]. [78]

---

78 Ibid., 86–87.

The ending corresponds to the dominantly apocalyptic view of the author who believed that the Messianic time was imminent. Of course, the equation of Kabbalah with true alchemy, which so distinctly makes an appearance here, should not come as much of a surprise to this author, since he has identified other disciplines he values such as astronomy or spherical trigonometry with the mysteries of Kabbalah as well. One can find an earlier passage about alchemy, albeit one less extreme in its formulation, in folio 9a-b. It serves as an explanation of Jacob's ladder in the Bible, on which the angels were ascending and descending:

> Great and mighty things will be revealed in the secret of the ladder, namely, how you will ascend in the secret of the ladder, and that is the secret of the verse: "and angels of God were going up and down on it" … and here the secret of nature will be revealed to you in the going up and down because the secret of the going up and down is the secret of the science of the Godhead. And herewith the secret of the upper [mystical] gold and silver and the secret of the lower [worldly] gold and silver will be revealed to you, as you can bring it forth in actuality and in nature out of all seven kinds of metals, and this is the true science of nature, which consists of the mystery of the ladder.

Measured against these astonishing comments by Taitaẓak, which anticipate the later identifications of the Christian kabbalists, statements of the sixteenth- and seventeenth-century kabbalists on metals using alchemical ideas represent a step backward. An overview of relevant examples makes this clear. *The Philosopher's Stone,* the title of a fictitious book allegedly written by Saadiah (ben Joseph) Gaon of Sura, and cited in the commentary on the *Sefer Yeẓirah* by Moses ben Isaac Botarel, a Spanish philosopher and kabbalist writing in Provence, proves only that Botarel knew about this alchemical concept from oral or written sources. (Botarel was notorious for his tireless inclination to invent titles and quotations from nonexistent books.) Around 1530, the Spanish kabbalist Meir ben Ezekiel ibn Gabbai, who was active in Egypt or Turkey, wrote an allegory about gold and silver to elucidate the two human drives toward good and evil.[79] He does not write about the transmutation of metals. I was unable to verify M. Güdemann's allegation that Zacharias the Hebrew (Prince Guizolfi), the founder of the Judaizing sect of Russia, who followed Prince Mikhail Olelkovich to Novgorod, was "much sought after for his ostensible knowledge about the Kabbalah and alchemy."[80] Naturally there is some mention of Jewish alchemists in the fifteenth century. The metal arts of a David Raby of Weiden, "extracted from the Hebrew," are mentioned in several later compilations on practical Kabbalah.[81] This is evidently a reference to Rabbi David from Vienna. In 1420, a Jewish alchemist named Salomo Teublein entered the service of the landgrave of Leuchtenberg.[82] In neither case, however, is there any mention of a connection to Kabbalah. In the narration of his wanderings in search of the Philosopher's Stone, Salomon Trismosin, the teacher of Paracelsus, recounts a meeting in Italy in 1480 with a Jew who understood German and practiced alchemy with an Italian tradesman. Their art, however, turned out to be fraudulent.[83] In 1482, a Marrano (Spanish crypto-Jew) from Játiva possessed not only magical books but also "Hebrew alchemical writings."[84]

---

79 See his *Avodat ha-Kodesh* I, 19.

80 See M. Güdemann, *Geschichte des Erziehungswesens und der Cultur der Juden* (Vienna, 1888), vol. 3, 156.

81 Ibid, op. cit., 155, as well as evidence from old *Segulot* manuscripts provided by M. Grunwald in several issues of the *Mitteilungen für jüdische Volkskunde*.

82 There is a report on this by G. Eis in *Ostbairische Grenzmarken: Passauer Jahrbuch* 1 (1957), 11–16.

83 Cf. *Splendor Solis: Alchemical Treatises of Solomon Trismosin Adept and Teacher of Paracelsus* (London, n.d.), 83.

84 F. Baer, *Die Juden im christlichen Spanien* (Berlin, 1936), part 1,

There are other sources that lead to Kabbalah, for instance, a text on the seven ranks of demons, from the sixteenth century, if not earlier, contained in a manuscript in the British Museum (Margoliouth, no. 845, fols. 89–94). There, in chapter 5, it is stated that the fifth king of demons, named Maqabai (!!), is also the jinnee of alchemy. It is quite possible that this text, like so many other treatises about the different ranks and princes of demons, originates from the early Middle Ages. The information in chapter 9, paragraph 3 of Moses Cordovero's 1548 kabbalist compendium *Pardes Rimmonim* (Cracow, 1592, fol. 69*a*) has kabbalist-alchemical characteristics. Here, in order to explain a certain passage in the *Sefer Yezirah,* Cordovero recites from an unnamed source a kind of alchemical process in which stone-like particles (most likely scale) are formed in heated, simmering water. Speculating on the *Zohar* passage discussed above (2:23*b*), the anonymous author of the *Gallei Rezayya,* written in 1552 (possibly in Safed), goes much further by addressing six of the metals discussed therein – gold, silver, iron, lead, copper, and tin – and their relationships to each other. He does not mention brass, which he did not seem to have understood; if he had, he would not have named iron as the *suspita* of gold. He explains the magical powers of the metallic Yadua bird, which is discussed in *Zohar* 3:184*b*, with the correct combination of the six metals used in its creation.[85] What is remarkable here is that the mixture of metals may produce impure powers that, as could be concluded, need to be overcome by separation.

Writing in 1570, Simeon Labi, the North African rabbi of Tripoli and author of *Ketem Paz* (Livorno, 1795), a barely explored,

---

vol. 2, 513.

85 Cf. the incomplete edition of the *Gallei Rezayya* (Mohilev, 1812), fols. 28*d*–29*a*. The alleged "Chaldean" sources of the story in the *Zohar* might be connected to the pseudo-Nabatean sources of the *Sefer ha-Tamar.* Both deal with the fabrication of oracle devices in the shape of a bird under the influence of astrological-alchemical views.

large commentary to the *Zohar,* is amiably inclined toward alchemy. About *Zohar* 1:249, mentioned above, he remarks:

> From this we can gather that nothing from the nat-
> ural sciences was concealed from the sages of the
> *Zohar.* Because they knew the cause and essence of
> all things, they also knew that nothing exists in the
> natural world without having roots in the upper
> [world] ... Know that gold and silver are identical ac-
> cording to the nature of their origin, their element
> and ore [?]. Pay no attention to those who say that
> they are two separate things. For they see that there
> is one mineral from which silver comes and one from
> which gold comes, and [thus] they say that there is a
> difference between them. But that is not so, for there
> is no difference between them except for their color,
> for the essence of gold is silver at first. And according
> to the places where silver comes into being, there are
> minerals that are exposed to the heat of the sun and
> as a result of their strong exposure, they become, in
> the course of time, red and turn to gold, for, as the
> heat increases, the white color changes and becomes
> red, just as you can see it happen with the fruits of
> trees; the side exposed to the sun turns red while the
> other side, not exposed, remains white or green, for
> the sun reddens or blackens or whitens according to
> the nature and disposition of each thing, and likewise
> for minerals. Those minerals that are exposed to the
> sun and facing in a southerly direction are colored
> red, while those that do not receive much heat from
> the sun remain white. [Thus] they are named [differ-
> ently] on earth: gold or silver, depending on the dif-
> ference of their location during the absorption of red
> color. You should know, however, that [in truth] they
> are *one* thing and undistinguishable, except in their
> location. Thus you find also that the wise men among
> the masters of alchemy do not concern themselves
> with other metals, nor do any work with them, but
> only with silver, to make it red, for those two metals
> exist on their own, but have a common origin, as we

were told by men of truth coming from Ophir [here perhaps East India?]. They found a mineral, which was half gold and half silver, because it did not ripen sufficiently under the warmth of the sun, and they melt it down to let each, gold and silver, come forth from it separately. And I am writing this in order to make known to you their [the sages'] wisdom, for nothing remains hidden to them.

Thus Simeon Labi thought something of alchemy. He even bends the kabbalist symbolism in favor of the alchemical one when he asserts, a few lines further down, "that the kabbalists, too, call gold, sun; and silver, moon."[86] This is, in fact, the symbolic language of the alchemists. His assertion regarding the kabbalists is, however, highly doubtful and, as far as I can see, is based solely on an allegorical reinterpretation of *Zohar* 1:249*b*, although that is certainly not its literal meaning. As we will see later, even the author of the *Esh Meẓaref,* who certainly would have been receptive to such ideas, has not dared to adopt the alchemical moon symbolism of silver. Not until two generations later did Abraham ben Mordecai Azulai, who, like Labi, was born in Fez, Morocco where alchemy played a large role, adopt this symbolism in his commentary to *Zohar* 3:184*b*, which talks about Balak's magical bird. Here, indeed, gold and silver are linked to the sun and the moon.[87] The passage in Azulai's commentary, however, seems to be derived from the *Zohar* commentary by Moses Cordovero, who does not mention such an association of silver with the moon in his dictionary of kabbalist symbolism (*Pardes Rimmonim,* chap. 23, fol. 151*c*).

---

86 See Labi, fol. 298*b*, for another pertinent passage on the mystery of colors in relation to the metals and the corruption of iron by "philosophers," e.g., alchemists.

87 See Azulai's *Zohar* commentary *Or ha-Ḥammah* (Przemysl, 1898), vol. 4, fol. 47*a*. Notations from the fourteenth century in MS Paris 806, fol. 97*b*, relate the moon and silver to each other symbolically.

Ḥayyim ben Joseph Vital, the most influential of Isaac ben Solomon Luria's disciples, has a completely different relationship to alchemy. About Luria we know nothing with certainty in this regard;[88] however, his disciple, who survived him by almost fifty years – he died in 1620 in Damascus – left several testimonies relevant to our discussion. In his autobiographical notes, which he assembled under the title *Sefer ha-Ḥezyonot* around 1610 and preserved in his own handwriting (the complete text was published in 1954),[89] Vital says that Luria saw the following sentence from Exodus 31:4 written on his forehead: "To make designs for work in gold, silver, and copper," to point "to my sins, that I have neglected the study of the Torah for two-and-a-half years while being occupied with the science of alchemy."[90] And in the preface to his much later

88 In *Sha'ar ha-Gilgulim* (Jerusalem, 1912), fol. 48a, Vital mentions the herb muscatella (Arabic, *akhil dhabab),* which "is able to bring about the alchemical [transmutation] to gold." He claims to have learned about several herbs from his teacher. Such an herb is also known elsewhere, albeit under different names, and seems to have originated in Arabic tradition. Abraham Chamoi (Abraham Shalom Hai), a collector of oriental-Jewish traditions, gives (around 1870) this account: "When I was young I wanted to gain knowledge in alchemy and its foundations, e.g., how through certain herbs tin and lead turn to gold. And this herb is called *Güldenkraut* [centaury; Latin, *centaurium minus*], in Arabic ḥashishat 'al-dhabab"; cf. his *Nifla'im Ma'asekha* (Livorno 1881), 24b. He refers to a passage from Vital's *Sha'ar Ru'aḥ-ha-Kodesh,* although it is not found there in its printed version. And the Jerusalem kabbalist Ḥayyim Joseph David Azulai mentions, in his collectanea *Midbar Kedemot* (Livorno, 1793), fol. 98c, an herb that can transform lead or gold to silver, "as we have been told by reliable authors."

89 I saw this manuscript in the spring of 1932 in Livorno. It was published after World War II by A.Z. Eshkoli from a poor microfilm copy (Jerusalem, 1954).

90 It is beyond comprehension why Eshkoli omitted this very passage, which is correctly included in earlier editions made of the autograph (such as Baghdad 1886, fol. 50a), from his edition of the *Sefer*

tractate on kabbalist ethics, *Sha'arei Kedusha,* Vital complains about people occupying themselves with things that mix good and devil, truth and lies, or that are generally null (*dewarim betelim*), by referring to (magical?) remedies, the science of alchemy, and the practice of using amulets and conjuration, without being specific about which category they belong to.[91] According to his "autobiography," *Shivḥei Rabbi Ḥayyim Vital,* the years he studied alchemy must have fallen between 1567 and 1569 (thus before he met Luria), since he speaks there of neglecting the study of the Torah for two-and-a-half years when he was twenty-four.[92] This statement can indeed be confirmed with another manuscript, without a doubt an autograph by Vital, wherein he collected magical practices and alchemical-metallurgical recipes. This important autograph was located for years in the invaluable kabbalist collection of Salomo Mussajow in Jerusalem, where I discovered it in 1930. The third part of the collection (fols. 34–45), written in eighty-three paragraphs in very dense but beautiful Sephardic script, deals with "chemical practices in matters of the seven metals." Here one finds a large number of detailed recipes of a purely chemical nature, which also contain much alchemical terminology. Perhaps one day the manuscript could be studied more closely from a photograph that was made at the time of its discovery.[93]

Even after Vital gave up his chemical practice of alchemy, he continued in his kabbalist writings to use the symbolism of metals, which diverges from the *Zohar* passage discussed

---

ha-Ḥezyonot, even though he refers to it in a footnote on page 1.

91 Thus in the preface to the first edition (Constantinople, 1734). Vital also proves to have general knowledge in chemistry in his *Sha'ar ha-Miẓvot* (Jerusalem, 1905), fols. 38*a* and 42*b*.

92 This is stated at the very beginning of his "autobiography."

93 The manuscript, which in 1943 was still on loan to the Jewish National Library in Jerusalem, together with the complete Mussajow collection, was lost after its return to the family.

above. Mercury, the leading substance of medieval and later alchemy, also appears here in its kabbalist illumination. It is the seventh metal, in place of the brass mentioned in the *Zohar*.[94] Vital symbolizes these seven metals (according to their rank: silver, gold, copper, tin, lead, mercury, iron) as the seven *sefirot* from *Ḥesed* to *Malkhut* and the seven planets in traditional sequence – a truly alchemical-astrological model.[95] Mercury belongs herein to the *sefirah Yesod* and thus to sexual symbolism. As C.G. Jung pointed out, the sexual significance of Mercury as Cupid can be found in some in medieval Latin visions.[96] There are no ramifications beyond it in Vital. His classification is definitely new, as mercury does not appear in any of the *sefirot* explanations of earlier generations. In one such tractate, *The Ladder of the Sefirot,* found in a manuscript in the British Museum (copied around 1500), the sequence of the metals is silver, gold, iron, tin, copper, brass (here simply called metal), lead.[97]

These developments take place first within the Spanish Kabbalah and later within the one coming out of Safed in the sixteenth century. In later times, there are two tendencies that

---

94 The long passage is in *Sefer ha-Likkutim* (Jerusalem, 1913), fol. 89b, which is attributed to Vital but is also in the kabbalistic compilation *Ḥesed le-Avraham* (of around 1630) by Abraham ben Mordecai Azulai, from an autograph of Vital on Psalms 84:7.

95 According to Vital, the forces of the four "spheres" or worlds of the Kabbalah, the *olamim,* are assigned to metals as well; the lowest of the worlds, *olam asiyyah* (the world of making), also called *olam kelippot* (the world of evil), is assigned to silver, while gold corresponds to the *olam beri'ah* (the world of creation); cf. Vital's *Arba Me'ot Shekel Kesef* (Cracow, 1886), fol. 9c-d. On the four worlds of the later Kabbalah, see my *Kabbalah* (New York, 1978), 116–22.

96 Cf. C.G. Jung, *Mysterium Coniunctionis*, 309f. Elsewhere in this book, quicksilver is distinctly female, whereas Mercury has a phallic aspect. Cf. also the corresponding symbolism in the *Esh Meẓaref,* discussed further below.

97 In MS British Museum (Margoliouth 1047), fol. 231.

demonstrate interest in alchemy in Jewish kabbalist circles. In the occidental Kabbalah of the seventeenth century, we have the comments of the Prague physician and kabbalist Abraham ben Shabbetai Sheftel Horowitz in his work *Shefa Tal*, printed in 1612. While generally explicating Cordovero's thoughts in great detail, in certain chapters not relevant here it falls back to the ideas of Luria. At the end of chapter 3 (fols. 6c–37d), there is a rather elaborate kabbalist theory of alchemy, wherein the doctrine of the transmutation of metals is developed "as it is known by the sages of alchemy," in relation to the interaction of all worlds and the *sefirot* itself. It also attempts a new reasoning for the priority of gold over silver, using the sixteenth-century doctrine of the four worlds, in which each of the ten *sefirot* is repeated according to its structure: the highest of these worlds, that of the emanations, is assigned to gold, while silver is the dominating symbol in the next lower world.[98] Between 1620 and 1640, Joseph Solomon Delmedigo, a Cretan from Candia who traversed Europe for many years and made a name for himself as a physician, kabbalist, and philosopher, authored many, mostly unpublished, texts.[99] The beginning of a treatise by Delmedigo on the Philosopher's Stone and the elixir of the philosophers is preserved in a manuscript at the Jewish Theological Seminary in New York. It was to have ten chapters, of which only the first seven pages survived.

Regarding the extent to which alchemy spread among the Jews of Morocco, there is evidence all the way up to the twentieth century. Even there, alchemy and Kabbalah often go hand in hand. A manuscript in the Gaster collection mentions a "scholar and saint" from Jerusalem who attempted the Great Work (Hebrew, *melakhah*).[100] In December of 1928 I saw,

---

98 A complete translation of this long passage is still needed.

99 On Delmedigo, see A. Geiger, *Biographie Josef Salomo del Medigo's* (Berlin, 1840), who rightly has pointed out the internal contradiction in the author's attitude toward Kabbalah.

100 The author explains the failure of the attempt with reflec-

in the Badhab manuscript collection in Jerusalem, a single folio, written around 1700 in Moroccan cursive script, which contains alchemical "tinctures" in Hebrew. Also around 1700, the Moroccan kabbalist Jacob Katan occupied himself with alchemy, about which he wrote a didactic poem in Arabic (using Hebrew letters), if we can believe Jacob Moses Toledano's identification of the author.[101] The manuscript, which I examined in January 1929, contains no Jewish material, only quotations by Arabic authors such as Jābir ibn Ḥayyān, Khālid ibn Yazīd, and Al-'Irāqī. I do not know the whereabouts of the treatise, which comprises almost fifty pages. An independent and thus twice as evidentiary testimony by an African Jew to the widespread alchemy of Morocco can be found in a report of the noted theologian Johann Salomo Semmler of Halle, of which I have only secondhand knowledge. A North African Jew, who visited Semmler in his last years, told him that alchemy was widespread among the Jews of Morocco. The rest of the conversation, however, appears to have been apocryphal gossip.[102]

In Jerusalem, at the end of 1924, I made the acquaintance of an octogenarian Moroccan scholar, Makhluf Amsellem (also known asAmsallam), who was a kabbalist, as well as a theoreti-

---

tions of a demonological nature; MS Gaster 1055 (now in the British Museum), fols. 42b–43a. Since the time of the destruction of the Temple the world became jumbled and thus also the natural relationships have become confused by demonic forces.

101 More of Jacob Katan's work can be found in Joseph ben Naim's *Sefer Malkhe Rabbanan* (Jerusalem, 1931), fol. 64a. The large manuscript described by M. Gaster in the *Jewish Encyclopedia*, vol. 1, 328ff., originated in Morocco around 1600.

102 I have only second-hand knowledge of this report from S. Rubin's very meager Hebrew text on alchemy, *Ebben ha-Ḥakhamim* (Vienna, 1874), 91–92. Rubin does not name his source, but it is probably the fourth or fifth issue of Semmler's *Unparteische Samm-lungen zur Historie der Rosenkreuzer* (Halle, 1788), of which I was only able to find the first two.

cal and practical alchemist. Amsellem showed me two large codices that he had compiled, one on Kabbalah, the other on alchemy. He told me that in his youth he had been the court alchemist for the sharif of Morocco. I later found proof of this in "Notes sur l'alchimie à Fes" (1906), an essay by G. Salmon, who by 1904 had seen Amsellem's codices in Fez. He reports therein that Amsellem became the court alchemist for Sultan Mulay Al-Ḥasan, who dedicated all of his spare time to the study of alchemy, albeit more for magical and occult purposes than in search of the Philosopher's Stone.[103] According to Amsellem, the sultan had collected about two thousand alchemical manuscripts and was trying to seize Amsellem's codices as well. The alchemical treatises I saw were in Arabic language but written in Hebrew letters. Shortly before his death, Amsellem began to print his kabbalist alchemical treatises, but he died in 1927 not long after his introduction (which I possess) had been set to type. I never found out what became of his manuscripts after his death.

---

103 G. Salmon, in the *Archives Marocaines,* vol. 7 (1906), 451-62. A visit with Amsellem in the year 1926 is recounted in *Die jiddische Stimme* (London, 1926), no. 2162. The article was previously published in the New York *Tag.*

Title page of the *Zohar* (Cremona, 1558)

II

arious sources, even those without any connection to Kabbalah, tell us about the interest of Italian Jews in alchemy. In the fifteenth century, in his didactic poem *Mikdash Me'at*, the poet Moses David ben Judah Rieti put alchemy at the top of his list of sciences under the Hebrew name *ḥokhmat ha-serefah* (20), a name I could not find in any other medieval literature. He makes no connection between Kabbalah, which he expatiates on afterward, and alchemy. At the end of the fifteenth century, one finds great enthusiasm for alchemy in a missive from the French Talmudist Jacob ben David Provençal to the Mantua scholar David ben Jehuda Messer Leon. Supposedly written in Naples in 1490, shortly before the expulsion of the Jews from Sicily (then part of Spain), the letter praises the study of the profane sciences. Remarkably, it consists almost entirely of fake quotations, apparently composed for the amusement of the author.[104] The author cites all kinds of fabricated excerpts on the sciences from the Palestinian Talmud, among others the following passage on alchemy allegedly from a commentary by the famous fourteenth-century Rabbi Asher ben Yechiel from Toledo on the tractate *Sheqalim*. Commenting on Ecclesiastes 7:12 ("For to be in the shelter of

---

104 Steinschneider was the first to point out – in the catalogue of the Bodleiana, col. 1248 – that these quotations were fabricated. Cf. also J.N. Epstein in *Hamaggid* (1902), 360 and 384. In *Monatsschrift für Geschichte und Wissenschaft des Judentums* 52 (1908), V. Aptowitzer calls the author of this text an imp, which is probably not far from the truth.

wisdom is to be also in the shelter of money, and the advantage of intelligence is that wisdom preserves the life of him who possesses it."), the rabbi is claimed to have written: "It is like the case of the rich from the House of Marqo'aya [literally, house of shreds] who were adept in the nature of the juices of gold and in peeling silver off dross." The alleged commentator understands perfectly well the meaning of this fictitious passage: "That family [of Marq'in] were alchemists and they caused the juices of certain herbs to congeal and made gold out of them. They also knew how to easily separate the dross from the silver. And this is a well-known science. However, they will not reveal the herbs, whose juices they congeal and turn into gold."[105] Based on the last sentence, it is unlikely that by "herbs" the author means simply those substances that come forth in the alchemical processes. Throughout his letter, Provençal continues to praise the high rank of alchemy within the natural sciences.[106] A sixteenth-century Hebrew manuscript in Oxford (Neubauer 1959, fols. 132–49), also from Italy, contains a "Book of Spagiric Art" – a common name for alchemy.

We know from a number of sources about a rabbi and alchemist by the name of Mordechai de Nello (or, according to another reference, de Nelle, which became distorted to de Delle), who came from the duchy of Milan but about whose career we know only from the time he spent in Poland, Bohemia, and Germany, where he must have stayed for some time since he not only wrote in German but composed many German-language poems, albeit awkwardly. De Nello is known as a follower of Paracelsus from a manuscript entitled *In Cementa et Gradationes Theophrasti Paracelsi Interpretatio Mordachij de Nelle Judæo* (identified by K. Sudhoff in Kassel). W.-E. Peuckert (from this source?) published a verse by de Nello, perhaps more of a

---

105 The Hebrew text of the letter is in the compilation *Dibre Ḥakhamim* (Metz, 1849; ed. Eliezer Ashkenazi), 68.

106 Ibid., 70.

dictum, in praise of Salomon Trismosin, the alleged teacher of Paracelsus, which sounds quite mystical:

> Study now where you are from
> And you will see who you are
> What you study, learn and are
> That is what you are of
> All that is outside of us
> Is also inside us, Amen.

Beneath the poem is a reference to de Nello's residence in Poland: "Mardocheus Nelle, Judæus, residing in Cracow in the year 1573." Either before or after his stay there, we find de Nello working as an alchemist in Dresden at the court of August I, the elector of Saxony, who reigned from 1553 to 1586. An avid and active adherent of alchemy, the elector had a magnificent laboratory built in Dresden, the so-called "Gold House." A manuscript preserved in the Dresden Archive, although only in an authentic copy from 1779, describes the manufacturing of "red-gold ore," that is, the red tincture of the alchemists. It also contains prophecies about the fate of the elector's successors. The elector is said to have written the following in the margin of the original manuscript: "We saw with our own eyes the works and labors made by Mardochai Rabbi de Nelle from red-golden ore and described hereafter. We spent, from beginning to end, 41 weeks on the entire work. August."[107] From Saxony, de Nello went to Prague, to the court of Emperor Rudolf II (1576–1612), an even more famous patron of alchemy and other occult disciplines. Among the alchemists, the emperor was called "the German Hermes Trismegistos." In Prague, de Nello again composed verses on the demise of a famous past alchemist. In these, there is no indication of any relationship of this adept to Jewish sources, let alone to the Kabbalah.

---

107 On August I and his court alchemists, see C. Kiesewetter, *Die Geheimwissenschaften* (Leipzig, 1895), 102–12.

The historically documented author Abraham ben David Portaleone of Mantua wrote his treatise *De auro dialogi tres* in Latin in 1583, and it was printed in Venice a year later.[108] Portaleone distinguished among three types of gold: vulgar gold, chemical gold, and divine gold, the latter of which was the exclusive domain of the kabbalists. Did he understand the symbolism of the kabbalists? As far as I can gather from the literature (I have not yet seen the original book), he does not go into any detail on the subject. Around the same time, Abraham Jagel, a Jew who later converted to Catholicism under the name of Camillo Jagel and worked as a censor, became interested in the connection of Kabbalah to alchemy, albeit without immersing himself very deeply into the kabbalist material.[109] Jagel refers to, among others, the previously mentioned writings of Abu Aflah, which had already been much quoted in *Likkutim*, the preserved manuscript of collectanea by the philosophizing kabbalist or "kabbalizing" philosopher Johanan Alemanno,[110] a contemporary and acquaintance of Pico della Mirandola.

It is worth mentioning here the alchemical interests of three generations of a prominent Jewish Italian family. Judah Aryeh, also known as Leone Modena from his Italian writings, was one of the most famous figures of his time. We know of his calamitous life from his own unusually frank, almost merciless autobiography – a testimony rare in Hebrew

---

108 Cf. L. Thorndike, *A History of Magic and Experimental Science* (New York, 1964, repr. of 1923ff. ed.), vol. 5, 645.

109 See Jagel's *Beth Ja'ar Lebhanon*, from which I.S. Reggio included excerpts in the *Kerem Ḥemed* (1836), vol. 2, 49–50.

110 Alemanno was interested not only in Kabbalah but in any and all occult knowledge, which his collectanea in MS Oxford, Neubauer 2234, clearly attests to. In this he resembles the members of the circle around Marsilio Ficino in Florence, which he was acquainted with and which held him in high esteem. On alchemy as a true science, see the introduction to his commentary on the Song of Songs, *Ḥeshek Shelomoh* (Halberstadt, 1860), fol. 36b, and the notices from the collectanea in the *Kerem Ḥemed*, 2, 48.

literature. He was an opponent of the Kabbalah. His uncle Shema'ya, who ran a pawnshop in Modena at the end of the sixteenth century, was attracted to alchemy, but it cost him his life; a Christian lured him, under false alchemical pretences and promises, into bringing him all the silver and gold from his shop and Shema'ya ended up murdered and robbed.[111] Modena (born 1571) was introduced to alchemy in 1603 by the physician Abraham di Cammeo, who twelve years later became Rabbi of Rome. Alchemy was an occupation, which according to Modena's own account, involved a great deal of money. In December 1614, Modena's oldest son, Mordecai, the object of his undivided love, turned full-time to alchemy at the expense of his Torah study, working with the highly adept Catholic priest Giuseppe Grillo in Venice. Modena writes:

> [Mordecai] exerted himself greatly, and became well versed in it to the point where all the masters of that science, who had become old and aged in it, marveled at what a youth like him knew of it. Finally, in the month of Iyar [spring 1615], he set up for himself a house in the *Ghetto Vecchio* [in Venice], and made all the preparations necessary for the Work, and he repeatedly performed there an experiment that he had learned and tried in the house of the priest, which consisted of making ten ounces of refined silver out of nine ounces of lead and one ounce of silver. And I saw this and tested it twice as it was done by him, and I myself sold the silver ... and I knew that it was true, even though it was a matter of great effort and exertion, and it required two and a half months each time. The end of the matter was that [we were able] to earn about a thousand ducats in a year. Nor was this all, for I too spent my life trying to understand

---

111 *Monatsschrift für Geschichte und Wissenschaft des Judentums* 38 (1894), 42; and in Modena's autobiography, *Sefer Ḥayyei Yehudah*, ed. Abraham Kahana (Kiev, 1911), 12.

such things, and I would not have misled myself had sin not caused it. During the feast of Sukkot 5376 [fall 1615], suddenly much blood flowed down from [Mordecai's] head to his mouth, and from then on he ceased performing that work, for they say perhaps the vapors and the smokes of the arsenics and the salts that enter into it injured his head. And he stayed thus for two years until his death, doing some easy things.[112]

I have quoted Modena's account at length because his description of his son's alchemical experiments may relate to the experiments of Rabbi Mordecai, discussed below, who also used arsenic in the making of silver.

An alchemical-kabbalist treatise that has survived in translations (the original is lost) and played a role in the non-Jewish alchemical literature after the work of Christian Knorr von Rosenroth is significant to our assessment and requires examination in the context of the interest of Italian Jews in alchemy. In his *Bibliotheca Hebræa* (Hamburg, 1721), Johann Christian Wolf lists the alchemical book *Esh Mezaref* (Purifying Fire), whose title he translates erroneously as *ignis purgans* rather than *ignis purgantis*, as it is in Malachi 3:2, where this "gold-smelting fire" is compared to the "Day of the Lord." As his source Wolf cites Dethlev Cluver, an author generally hostile toward alchemy who discusses the text in his *Historische Anmerckungen über die nützlichsten Sachen der Welt* from 1706 (172ff). I was not able to inspect this rare book until 1979 in Berlin. In it are several excerpts from Knorr von Rosenroth's book, which will be mentioned below (172–75). However, the title of the essay, "The Gilden Kabbalah of the Jews: How

112 Ibid., 30 (from 1603) and 34 (from 1614). A letter written by Modena to Abraham Cammeo on the subject of magic in 1605 is printed in L. Blau, *Leo Modenas Briefe und Schriftstücke* (Strasbourg, 1907), 83–84. [English translation taken from R. Patai, *The Jewish Alchemists* (Princeton, 1994), 400 – Trans.]

to Transform Metals According to the Sefirot to Create Gold and Silver," does not correspond to the content of the book, in which the ten sefirot play only a symbolic role in relation to metals and are not applied directly to the process of making gold. Cluver also claims that Jews hold this book in such high esteem that no Christian is worthy of knowing its content or reading it. As evidence for this he cites that "not long since" an "insolent Jew" had uttered this very opinion "all around the exchange" – probably in Hamburg, where Cluver worked. And what mythology – after all, Cluver himself received all his knowledge from a Christian source!

Knorr von Rosenroth quite surprised the Christian world when he announced on the title page of the first volume of his *Kabbala Denudata* ("Kabbalah Unveiled"; Sulzbach, 1677) that it included, among other texts, a "Compendium of the kabbalist-alchemical book *Esh Meẓaref*, about the Philosopher's Stone, etc."[113] This announcement must have attracted the attention of anyone interested in alchemy. H. Kopp, the only historian of alchemy who until then had been troubled by this book, wrote that he looked for the text in vain in the first part of *Kabbala Denudata*.[114] But this famous scholar did not search thoroughly enough; moreover, he took false comfort from his misunderstanding of a note in the alchemical book *Kompass der Weisen* (1782) – which he thought indicated that the text was mingled together with the *Zohar* and was thus unrecognizable. In fact, the first twenty quotations stand out clearly and are for the most part literal translations of the first eight chapters of *Esh Meẓaref*. Knorr von Rosenroth could rightfully claim to have provided a compendium of this work, as the major parts are all included, albeit "split up," or dispersed among various places. The quotations are located in the first volume:

---

113 *Compendium Libri Cabbalistico-Chymici, Aesch Mezareph dicti, de Lapide Philosophico.*

114 H. Kopp, *Die Alchemie in älterer und neuerer Zeit* (Heidelberg, 1886), vol. 2, 233.

116–18 (generalia, from chap. 1); 151–52 (gold); 185 (tin); 206–7 (iron); 235 (on Gehazi, the servant of Elisha, from chap. 1); 241 (sulfur); 271–72 (copper); 301–5 (gold); 345–46 (lead); 359–60 (silver); 430 (on the dove as a preparatory stage of the Work); 441–42 (quicksilver); 455 (on the river Jordan as an alchemical symbol); 456 (silver); 483–85 (silver); 570 (copper); 625–26 (lead); and 683–84 (iron).

There remains the question of the character and authenticity of these fragments. The wording and content quite clearly indicate that Knorr von Rosenroth was working from a Hebrew source, not from Latin or any other language. In his literal, albeit not always correct translation, the Hebrew language shines through the non-chemical passages (about which I cannot form any opinion).[115] From Knorr von Rosenroth's rendering of the technical term *transmutatio* (548) with the Hebrew *tseruf* (combination) we may presume that the original author used this word.[116] Wordplays such as equating *Yesod* with quicksilver (441) – for it is the *fundamentum totius artis transmutatoriæ* (the foundation of the whole art of transmutation) – presup-

---

115 E.g., the Hebrew phrases כתבתי זה אני הקטן (I, 303) and עכשיו וכיד ה'הטובה עלי מצאתי מה שאני מלמדך (I, 304); I, 456 uses *materia operis* for *khomer ḥa-melakhah* – yet more evidence of the usage of *melakhah*.

116 He may also have used the Hebrew *temura* in this technical sense, which Knorr von Rosenroth translated in several places with *transmutatio.* In other writings, the verb *haphakh* is used in the sense of transmuting. *Mahapekhata ha-mattekhoth* is used in an alchemical manuscript in the Staatsbibliothek Berlin as a translation of *transmutatio,* as Steinschneider noted in his *Verzeichnis der hebräischen Handschriften,* Zweite Abteilung (Berlin, 1897), 120. This collection of various alchemical texts and excerpts does not date back further than the mid-seventeenth century, since it cites writings by Joseph Solomon Delmedigo (on p. 121), and may, in fact, originate from a disciple of Delmedigo's. Abraham ben Mordecai Azulai also uses this verb in that sense. Aloisius Wiener (von Sonnenfels) uses the verb *shinnah* for "he transmuted" (e.g., on p. 107) in the Hebrew sections of his *Splendor Lucis* (Vienna, 1744). Likewise, Knorr von Rosenroth used *alterare* on his frontispiece.

pose a Hebrew text. The author, who was well versed in the Talmud, understood Latin, as is evident from his explanation of the word *aspirkha* as quicksilver, following Rashi's commentary (in the *Gemara*, tract. Gittin, fol. 69*b*), for it is equal to *aqua sphærica quia e sphæra mundana profluit* (spherical water that flows from the mundane sphere). *Sphærica* with an *alef prostheticum* would certainly conform to this Hebraic word image if one were to confuse the consonants *kaf* and *qof,* as is frequently the case in Hebrew with foreign words. Thus a correct explanation is here supported by an incorrect reading. [117]

The content of the text speaks even more clearly. The first chapter apparently contained an introduction, from which arguably the main part is quoted; the order of the second through the eighth chapters is clear. The text – it is not apparent whether it contained any more chapters – was arranged by metals, in the following sequence: gold, silver, iron, tin, copper, quicksilver, and sulphur. It had three parts: a purely kabbalist part pertaining to the mystical symbolism of metals and their relation to the *sefirot* (incidentally, without quoting the *Zohar* more than once); a purely chemical part recounting certain processes and operations, essentially without any relation to the other parts; and finally an astrological part, evidently at the end of each chapter, which describes the planetary amulets of the respective metals. This latter part provides relevant information about the origin of the text and is related, more or less serendipitously, to the first by way of the unrestrained use of gematria (numerology).

The introduction presents Elisha, the disciple of the Prophet Elijah, as "an exemplar of natural wisdom and a despiser of worldly goods," which is taken (I, 117 and 151) from an

---

117 The reading with the consonant ר (*resh*), which is already old and even used in the Talmud MS Munich, Hebr. 95, is based on a misreading of the graphically very similar consonant ד (*dalet*). The correct form was *aspedikha.*

interpretation of an episode (on Na'aman) in 2 Kings 5:6. This is followed by a synopsis of the chapters to come:

> But know that the mysteries of this [chemical] wisdom do not differ [or, are not far] from the supernal mysteries of the Kabbalah. For just as there is a reflection of predicaments [prædicamenta] in [the side of] sanctity, so there is also in impurity. And the sefirot, which are in the Aziluth [the highest world] are also in the asiyyah [the lowest world], yes even in that kingdom commonly called Minerals, though on the supernal [region] its excellence [excellentia] is by all means greater. Therefore the place of Keter [the first sefirah] is here occupied by the metallic root [radix metallica], which contains nature, deeply concealed and in great darkness, and from which all metals have their origin. Thus Keter is concealed and from it emanate all the other sefirot. Lead takes the place of Ḥokhma. Just as Ḥokhma stand closest to the sefirah Keter, so lead emerges out of the radix metallica directly; and in another, similar allegorical depiction [ænigmatibus] it is called [like Ḥokhma] the "father" of the subsequent natures [naturæ].[118] Tin takes the place of Binah, which shows its its rigor and judicial severity by its grayness, which resembles the hair of old men, and by its gnashing.[119] Silver is related by all the masters of the Kabbalah to Ḥesed, primarily because of its color and use. To this also belong the whitish substances. Then follows the red. Gold is placed under the Gevurah in the most common opinion of the kabbalists. According to Job 37:22, it is also related to the North, less for its color than for

---

118 Lead seems to be considered here one of the symbols for the prima materia.

119 Gnashing appears in the Bahir as a vowel symbol of the strict Judgment (par. 28). Here it is applied to the so-called "tin cry," which is already mentioned in the alchemical book Emek ha-Melekh, mentioned above, fol. 3b. [If a bar of tin is bent, it will "cry" as the crystal structure is disrupted. – Trans.]

its heat and sulphur. Iron is related to *Tif'eret,* which is also called, according to Psalm 2:12, *Z'ir Anpin* (the Impatient One).[120] *Netsaḥ* and *Hod* are the place of the androgynous copper, just as the two pillars in the Temple of Solomon, which were made of copper according to 1 Kings 7:15, are related to these two modes. *Yesod* is quicksilver, for this *sefirah* is given especially the surname *ḥay* (living).[121] Finally, the "medicine of metals" [see below] is related to *Malkhut,* because, among many reasons, it represents the two remaining natures under the metamorphosis of both gold and silver, the right or the left side, judgment or mercy. Of all this more will be said elsewhere [in this book?]. Thus I have handed you the key to unlock most of the closed gates and have opened the door to the innermost sanctums of nature.[122] But if anyone wishes to arrange this [order] differently, I will not be in opposition to him, for all is tended to one truth. For it could be said that the three upper [*sefirot*] are the wellspring of all things metallic. "Thick" water [the *prima materia*] would be *Keter;* salt, *Ḥokhma;* sulphur, *Binah.* The lower seven

---

120 This is common symbolism in the *Zohar,* especially in the two *Idroth* (the *Idra rabba* and the *Idra zuta*). What the Christian kabbalists mistranslated as *macro-anthropos,* or the Great Primordial Man, is in fact, in the original *Zohar,* the "Patient One," the uppermost *sefirah* in which the forces of strictness do not exist, as opposed to the "Impatient One," where these forces do exist.

121 In the Kabbalah, especially with Joseph Gikatilla, the biblical name of God, *El Ḥay* (the living God), is considered to belong to *Yesod.* In the *Zohar* and in Gikatilla, quicksilver (Hebrew, *kessef ḥay*) is not present, but already Vital justified this allocation of quicksilver to *Yesod* (see n. 95).

122 I found a similar phraseology in the *Cœlum Terrae* by Thomas Vaughan (Eugenius Philalethes), almost at the end of the book: "If thou doest know the First Matter know also for certain, thou hast discovered the sanctuarie of Nature; there is nothing between thee and her treasures, but the doore: that indeed must be opened." Vaughan, *Magical Writings,* op. cit., 152.

> [*sefirot*] would represent the seven metals: namely,
> *Gedullah* [*Ḥesed*] and *Gevurah,* silver and gold; *Tif'eret,*
> iron; *Netsaḥ* and *Hod,* tin and copper; *Yesod,* lead;
> *Malkhut* [in such a system], the metallic feminine and
> the "moon of the wise," also the field into which are
> sowed the seed of the secret minerals, and as is im-
> plied, the gold water, as is written in Genesis 36:39.
> But know this, my son, that mysteries are hidden
> herein that no human's tongue can utter. Therefore
> I shall no longer sin with my tongue but hold my
> mouth at bay. (*Kabbala Denudata,* 1:116–18)

My impression is that not much is missing from this introduction and that it may have had a complimentary closing.
A few remarks on this long quotation are in order. The first
scheme, in which everything is pretty much jumbled together,
does not conform to any known *sefirah* symbolism or alchemical ranking of metals. That the highest *sefirot* also encompasses
lead and tin seems very artificial and scarcely comprehensible
in kabbalist terms. The sefirah *Ḥesed* is hereunder quicksilver
and understood as metal and a symbol of male sexuality. This
corresponds to several sources, which I have cited above.[123] No
less striking is the assertion of the androgynous nature of copper, for which I could not find any evidence in the alchemical
literature, even though it may be explained by the symbolism
of the two copper temple pillars. The "medicine of metals" is
a common name used by the alchemists for the Philosopher's
Stone. It evidently derives its meaning from the alleged power
of the stone to transmute sick (e.g., base) metals into precious
ones.[124] On the other hand, there is a contradiction when, ac-

---

123 See note 95.

124 Cf. H. Silberer, 75. This term is in use by the fifteenth century by Simeon ben Ẓemaḥ Duran, in his *Magen Avot,* fol. 10a. Another
symbolism of the *Esh Meẓaref* for *Malkhut* is "Red Sea," from which can
be extracted the Salt of Wisdom, *sal sapientiæ,* and across which the
ships of Solomon fetched gold (*Kabbala Denudata,* 1:346).

cording to the much more plausible second scheme, *Malkhut* is described with overt symbols of the *prima materia*. In the eighth chapter (*Kabbala Denudata,* 1:456), the moon of the sages is referred to expressly as *materia operas* (material for the Work). At the same time, the moon is called "a medicine leading to white" because it "receives its white splendor from the sun." This second scheme is remarkable in two respects. The differentiation of the three upper *sefirot,* which themselves are not metals but the wellspring of all things metallic, from the lower seven, which are actually six metals together with the *prima materia,* may prove that the author had already been under the influence of the innovations brought about by Paracelsus, who considered salt, in addition to quicksilver and sulphur, such a basic element (here called wellspring) of all metals.

In the sixteenth and seventeenth centuries, the so-called "thick water" is sometimes the surname of Mercury, or quicksilver, and sometimes that of chaos or *prima materia,* which of course can mean the same thing. It is unclear how the author envisaged the connections between the last *sefirah,* which he equated so unambiguously with the *prima materia* of alchemy, and the first *sefirah,* which belongs to the wellsprings of metals.[125]

Secondly, there is in this scheme the bizarre interpretation of Genesis 36:39 with respect to the purification of quicksilver. This verse, which in the Torah ends the enumeration of

---

125 There are long elaborations on the equivalence of the *prima materia* to chaos and quicksilver, as well as "thick water," especially in the writings of Thomas Vaughan, e.g., in *Magia Adamica* and *Lumen de Lumine.* I could not ascertain whether these symbolisms are in the 1597 book on hylic chaos by the German alchemist Heinrich Khunrath. Another term found in the *Esh Meẓaref* but almost certainly not in Jewish sources is *Kabbala naturalis* (*Kabbala Denudata,* 1:449). I suspect that it originates in Paracelsus, which might also be the source for the term *gur* (derived from the Hebrew word for lion cub and popular with the Christian kabbalists of the sixteenth and seventeenth centuries) for "matter of the metallic medicine," i.e., the *prima materia.*

the Edomite kings (who reigned even before the Israelites in Edom) with the naming of the wife of the last of these kings, has a long and curious history (which cannot be expounded upon here [126]). The passage reads: "And [King] Baal-Hanan son of Achbor died, and Hadad reigned in his stead; and the name of his city was Pau and the name of his wife was Mehetabel, daughter of Matred, daughter of Me-Zahab." The second name of the father, Me-Zahab, literally "gold water," suggests an alchemical interpretation, as in the following dismissive remark by Abraham ibn Ezra from his twelfth-century commentary: "Some find here an intimation of those who make gold from copper, and these are idle and empty chatter." In point of fact, the word me-zahab was used in Hebrew around 1400 as an alchemical equivalent to gold water. [127]

In addition to the author of the Esh Meẓaref, another Jewish scholar, Benjamin ben Immanuel Mussafia, a physician and philologist well known in his time, published a Latin text in

---

126 In Zohar 1:145b it says that Rabbi Joḥanan ben Sakkai gave three hundred interpretations on this verse; the same is written in the Midrash ha-Ne'elam in the Zohar Ḥadash, fol. 6d–7a. One such mystical interpretation is in the Idra rabba in Zohar 3:135b and 142a, which played a large role in the history of the Kabbalah. The verse from Genesis incited much speculation among the mystics. In his article on alchemy in the Encyclopædia Judaica, vol. 2, col. 543, B. Suler speculates that the name Mehetabel might have reminded the alchemists of the Greek word metabolé for transmutation. I find this unlikely.

127 Bereshith rabba about Genesis 36:39 (ed. Theodor, 999–1000, par. 83.4), as well as a parallel passage in the first Targum Yerushalmi. "What is gold and silver to me!" the rich father is supposed to have exclaimed. In the second Targum Yerushalmi it says, however, that Matred, the father of Mehetabel, was a goldsmith who became rich, etc. And the thirteenth-century Yemenite author of the Midrash Haddadol ha-Gadol (ed. M. Margulies; Jerusalem, 1947) I, 615, says that Matred was the world's first goldsmith, without referring to the next name, Me-Zahab. Using this as his source, Nathaniel ibn Jesaja, also from Jemen, developed in 1327 the thesis that Matred was an alchemist; cf. his Nūr aẓ-ẓulam (ed. Kafiḥ; Jerusalem, 1957, Arabic), 156.

praise of alchemy. Titled *Mezahab epistola* (Hamburg, 1640), the text deals at great length with the alchemical interpretation of this verse. *Mezahab* is the *aurum potabile* (potable gold) of the alchemists. The author seeks to deduce the importance of Jews in alchemy from the Bible and, for this purpose, rather arbitrarily consults numerous biblical passages and later sources. In doing so, he also uses an alchemical interpretation of the Golden Calf, a popular motif with Christian alchemists of the time. [128] I did not find a connection to the *Esh Meẓaref*, the author of which deviates from his own scheme of assigning the elements to the *sefirot* whenever his symbolism becomes too tight. Then its strange and ingrafted character becomes obvious. Thus he has to assign tin to the *sefirah Netsaḥ* and gold to *Tif'eret*, in order to sustain the alchemical symbolism of the sun and accommodate gold's status as the "most perfect of stones." While the sun remains bound in the Kabbalah to this *sefirah*, gold is always assigned to the strict Judgment. The moon symbolism of silver had to be completely abandoned by him since, in the Kabbalah, it represents the last *sefirah Malkhut* and can

---

128 The very rare text by Mussafia is reprinted and discussed in Johann Jakob Schudt's *Jüdische Merckwürdigkeiten* (Frankfurt, 1714), vol. 3, 329–39. It contains no alchemical material. A more extensive commentary on Mussafia's epistle can be found in Johann Ludwig Hannemann's *Ovum Hermetico-Paracelsio-Trismegistum, id est Commentarius Philosophico-Chemico-Medicus in quandam Epistolam Mezahab dictum de Auro* (Frankfurt, 1694). I was able to leaf through a copy of this 400-page book in London in July 1927 and found no material relevant to Jewish alchemy. Curious in regard to Mussafia's motif of the alchemically-understood Golden Calf is a book I saw in America in 1938: *Moses Güldenes Kalb / nebst dem magischen Astralischen-Philosophischen-absonderlich dem cabalistischen Feuer / vermittelst welchem letzteren Moses / der Mann Gottes / dieses güldene Kalb zu Pulver zermalmet / aufs Wasser gestäubet und den Kindern Israel zu trinken gegeben* (Frankfurt, 1723). The author does not refer to Mussafia; instead, he draws amply on the first volume of the *Kabbala Denudata* in order to give his book a kabbalist gloss.

in no way be related to *Ḥesed,* toward which the silver symbolism of the Kabbalah tends. In any case, gold does not occupy an overly significant place in the whole scheme, since the author generally yields to this symbolism. Nor does he have any particular reason to emphasize it, and one can understand why he cites and teaches only one of the chemical practices, the transmutation to attain silver. The process, which he describes in detail, partly in chemical terms, and partly in alchemical symbols, is to take about four months.

In *Re metallica de argento,* Knorr von Rosenroth cites the work of a Rabbi Mordecai, from the third chapter of the *Esh Meẓaref* (1:483–85). B. Suler identifies him as Mordecai, the son of Leone Modena who transmuted lead to silver and perished from alchemical processes. If the assumption that Modena's son left behind writings of his own were indeed correct, our text would have to be dated between 1620 and 1660, and Knorr von Rosenroth would have gotten hold of it not long after it was written. Nothing else, however, speaks for such a late date. We know with certainty only that the author used the Cremona edition of the *Zohar* (1560), since he refers to its pagination.[129] He was moved by a passage at the end of the *Zohar* on the responsibility of the true physician to search "occult books" for the mysteries of the healing of creatures by means of alchemy. Only a historian of alchemy could determine whether an analysis of the chemical processes described in the text would help to date it more precisely. I am unable to identify them in other writings; in any case, they represent the typical mixture of scientific and mystical alchemy. In terms of its terminology, the Hebrew text of the quote, likely of Italian origin, should be highly interesting; however, I have not been able to reconstruct it completely. At the end, Mordecai adds the following: "This should be compared to the writings of the Arab philosopher, for he dealt with arsenic in greater detail." Indeed,

---

129 *Kabbala Denudata,* 1:303.

arsenic plays an important part in this process. The Arab philosopher is not Jābir ibn Ḥayyān (Latin, *Geber*) but rather Ibn Sīnā (Latin, *Avicenna*). *De anima in arte alchymiæ,* a rather elaborate text that was attributed to him, deals at length with the "four spirits," one of which is arsenic.[130] Rabbi Mordecai may have known the Latin translation of this book. That he knew Latin is evident from his discussion of the Latin name for the planet Jupiter (Hebrew, *tsedeq*), which was forbidden to be uttered because of its derivation from a pagan cult. His explanation of iron combines Kabbalah with alchemy in its symbolism:

> This metal is the middle line reaching from one end to the other [in the Kabbalah, this is a definition of the *sefirah Tif'eret*]. Here it is that male and bridegroom, without whom the virgin cannot be impregnated. This is the "sun of the wise," without whom the moon would be in perpetual darkness. He who knows its rays works in daylight; the others grope in the night.[131]

I do not understand the alchemical exposition of lead and sulphur.[132] Elsewhere, he assumes that the alchemical symbolism of the green, red, and black lion is known.[133] It is impossible for me to determine the age of the text, except for the speculation that the here mentioned Rabbi Mordecai is the son of Leone Modena. I have already demonstrated that the

---

130 According to Lippmann, op. cit., 368 and 407.

131 *Kabbala Denudata,* 1:206.

132 *Kabbala Denudata,* 1:185–86. It reads: "In particular transmutations, its sulphurous nature does not come forth, but together with other sulphurs, especially of the red metals [i.e., iron and copper], it reduces 'thick water' [the *materia prima*], if duly terrified into gold, so also into silver, if it is carried over into the subtle nature of 'thin water' by quicksilver, which can easily be done also with tin." According to 345, lead is also regarded as the primordial salt (*sal primordialis*).

133 *Kabbala Denudata,* 1:151–52.

text cannot have been written before 1560. While the author was familiar with the migration of alchemists through the four worlds in the later Kabbalah, he makes no mention of the specific ideas of the Lurian Kabbalah that began to spread from Italy in the beginning of the seventeenth century. The unrestrained use of gematria, even in its most excessive forms, would point to a later date, while the form the book takes of addressing a disciple, which was used less frequently by later kabbalists, would suggest an earlier date. It is also important to consider the third, astrological part of the book. Knorr von Rosenroth's source provides the magic-square *camea* (amulet) for each metal, with the numbers referring to the corresponding planet.[134] This conforms to the classical astrological tables; however, most of the actual squares differ from those found in the older astrological magic of the Middle Ages, preserved in a Hebrew manuscript (Munich 214, fols. 145–46). I have arranged the table of these correlations below according to the traditional planetary system, not the kabbalist system of the *sefirot*:

Planet	Row Number of the Magic Square	Metal	*Sefirah*	*Sefirah* of metals in Vital
Saturn	3	lead	Ḥokhma	Hod
Jupiter	4	tin	Binah & Netsah	Netsaḥ
Mars	5	iron	Tif'eret	Malkhut
Sun	6	gold	Gevurah & Tif'eret	Gevurah
Venus	7	copper	Hod	Tif'eret
Mercury	8	quicksilver	Yesod	Yesod
Moon	9	silver	Ḥesed	Ḥesed

---

134 Cf. *Kabbala Denudata*, 1:271, 304, 359, 443, 625, 677, and 684.

It becomes clear from this table that Knorr von Rosenroth's symbolism did not originate in kabbalist circles, where the sequence of the *sefirot* would have undoubtedly determined the numerical order of the squares, but rather in astrological circles, where the order of the planets is determined by their reverse proximity to the earth, as it was understood at the time. Evidently this was done with conscious, systematical intent. Already the fact that Saturn is here related to Ḥokhma while the *Tiqqunei ha-Zohar* (around 1300), for instance, related it to the lowest *sefirot Yesod* or *Malkhut* attests to its incompatibility with the old *sefirah* symbolism of the Kabbalah.[135] I believe, however, that the origin of these planetary amulets can be determined with certainty. They only penetrated Jewish circles through the well-known book by Cornelius Agrippa of Nettesheim, *De Occulta Philosophia*, which was published in its entirety for the first time in Cologne in 1533, a date that accords with the assumed date of the *Esh Meẓaref.* The subsequent editions, published in Paris (1567) and Lyon (1600), found an especially large readership. Agrippa introduces this entire symbolism (with the exception of the sun), exactly as found in our text, for the first time into wide circles of the Occident, although it had been known since the fourteenth century. He dedicates an entire chapter (chapter 22 of book 2) to it. He quotes neither directly from the Arabs, from whom it likely derives, nor from the kabbalists, but simply from "magical books", that is, from manuscripts related to the magical text *Picatrix* (*Ghâyat al-Hakîm fi'l-sihr*).[136] Had he used kabbalist

---

135 In this way, the two passages on Saturn in *Tiqqunim* 70, fol. 121*b* and 132*b*, are understood by Jacob Ẓevi ben Naphtali Jolles in his lexicon of kabbalist symbolism *Kehillat Ya'akov* (Lemberg, 1870), s.v. *shabtai.*

136 On magical squares and the borrowing of this system in the Occident from the Arabs, cf. A. Warburg, *Gesammelte Schriften* (Leipzig and Berlin, 1932), vol. 1, 528; the major study by W. Ahrens in *Islam* 7 (1916), 186–240, especially 197–203; and finally the valu-

sources, an author such as Agrippa, who was obsessed with the Kabbalah, would not have failed to allude to that fact. Agrippa's planetary characteristics are completely unfamiliar to Jews and were likely invented by him. On the Jewish side, we have the Sicilian Rabbi Nissim Abulfarash, the father of Flavius Mithridates (Gugliem Raimundus Moncada),[137] the famous translator of kabbalist and Arabic texts, who attests to his having practiced magic. He also had a gold amulet of the sun made, depicting, on one side, the typical image of a lion, and on the other, a magic square that, according to Agrippa's table and earlier Arabic sources, represented Saturn. The contradiction to the systemization of numerical squares according to the planetary order is evident here. This Sicilian rabbi, possibly of Egyptian or Syrian descent, did not yet know the later scheme. There is no evidence that the author of the *Esh Mezaref* understood Arabic and drew directly on Arabic sources. That he understood Latin has already been demonstrated above. Had he been under the influence of a Latin source, it would have been that of Agrippa, if not a later one. Indeed our text seems to be the only book that assimilates Agrippa's ideas. Since it had limited distribution and left no trace in the Jewish literature, it may be said that it was premature of authors such as Athanasius Kircher in *Œdipus Ægyptiacus* (published in 1653, a quarter-century before the publication of the *Kabbala Denudata*) and others after him to pass these

---

able material in the facsimile of the 1533 edition, published by K.A. Nowotny (Graz, 1967), especially 430–33 and 906–8.

137 On Flavius Mithridates, an extraordinarily learned convert, see U. Cassuto in *Zeitschrift für die Geschichte der Juden in Deutschland* 5 (1934), 230–36; and Ch. Wirszubski's comprehensive analyses of Mithridates's kabbalist translation in his *Pico della Mirandola's Encounter with Jewish Mysticism* (Cambridge, Mass., 1989). [See also the introduction by G. Busi in the first volume of the complete Kabbalist Library of Giovanni Pico della Mirandola, *The Great Parchment. Flavius Mithridates' Latin Translation, the Hebrew Text, and an English Version* (Berlin and Florence, 2004), 13–48. – Trans.]

planetary amulets off as kabbalistic.[138] The author of the *Esh Mezaref* himself nowhere characterizes his text as kabbalistic. All but one of the magic squares cited by him match those of Agrippa: the square of the sun, namely, of gold. Here the author substitutes 111, the sum of the numerical row, with the sum 216 in order to emphasize the relation to the lion, the symbol of strength and the *sefirah Gevurah*. The Hebrew word for lion, *arye,* has the numerical value 216. Thus Agrippa's scheme was changed in one detail in favor of the *sefirah* symbolism.

Thus we seem to be dealing in this text with a kabbalist-alchemical syncretism, the use of which one would not put past a learned Italian Jew from the time between the years 1570 and 1650. Following the prevailing kabbalist symbolism, the text, as mentioned before, speaks less about the making of gold than the general transmutation of metals and, specifically, the creation of pure silver from impure base metals. The various kabbalist, chemical, and astrological elements are only loosely connected. This singular attempt to connect the three shows more than anything else how little they have in common and how difficult it is to link specific aspects of kabbalist symbolism with alchemical-astrological symbolism (as we have seen above with Joseph Taitazak). In my judgment, this rather inept attempt speaks as much against the existence of a true kabbalist-alchemical tradition and tendency among Jews as it attests to the strength of non-Jewish influences on individual kabbalists, which would be most probable in Italy.

Except for Knorr von Rosenroth, no one knew about this text. The assertion of the English theosopher and occultist W.W. Westcott, who belonged to the circle around Madame Blavatsky, that the *Esh Mezaref* still existed in a Hebrew or rather Aramaic-Chaldean text as a special tractate merits no credence.

---

138 Kircher describes these planetary squares in detail in his *Arithmologia sive de abditis numerorum mysteriis* (Rome, 1665).

The fate of Knorr von Rosenroth's copy can no longer be ascertained; it is not in his estate, the major part of which was given to his friend Franciscus Mercurius van Helmont. It is certain that those authors who wrote after him only knew the book from the *Kabbala Denudata*. For those friends of alchemy who could not afford Knorr von Rosenroth's expensive Latin *Opus magnum*, or perhaps did not read Latin, an anonymous author who called himself "A Lover of Philalethes" made an English translation entitled *A Short Enquiry Concerning the Hermetick Art. Address'd to the Studious Therein ... to which Is Annexed, a Collection from Kabbala De-nudata, and Translation of the Chymical-Cabbalistical Treatise, Intituled Æsch-Mezareph; or, Purifying Fire*. Published in London in 1714, the book contains the Latin text of the fragments as well as their English translation.[139] In a copy at the Jewish National Library in Jerusalem, the original owner, Daniel Cohen d'Azevedo, a contemporary who belonged to the Portuguese Jewish community of London, wrote that he received his book from the author who he identified as Robert Kellum. A reprint, revised and in some places corrected, was published by Westcott under the pseudonym "Sapere Aude," with a preface in which he writes about the book:

> The Æsch Mezareph is almost entirely alchymical in its teachings, and is suggestive rather than explanatory in its words. The allegorical method of teaching runs through it, and the similes have to be kept carefully in mind, otherwise confusion will result. Several alchymic processes are set out, but not in such a way that they could be carried out by a neophyte; any attempt to do so would discover that something vital was missing at one stage or other.[140]

---

139 I. Macphail, *Alchemy and the Occult* (New Haven, 1968), vol. 2, 514.

140 W. W. Westcott, *Collectanea Hermetica*, vol. 4: (London, 1894).

Since the text no longer existed in its entirety, it should be no surprise that pseudoepigraphy soon set in. The impossible assertions in their titles alone speak for their inauthenticity and for belonging to the eighteenth century. Many of the manuscripts were offered for sale in the 1786 catalogue of the Viennese book dealer Rudolf Gräffer. In this catalogue, a commentary on the compendium of *Esh Meẓaref* (with a preface) was offered, written by Leander de Meere, an otherwise unknown author. There is also a *Golden Kabbalah of Jews As Well As Instructions of the Sefirot About How the Transmutation of Metals Is To Come About,* which seems to go back to Cluver's title. The pretentiousness of this title is nothing compared to the mysterious text that J.K. Huysmans invented in the sixth chapter of his novel *Là-Bas,* where a great Satanist "took from one of the shelves of the library a manuscript which was none other than the Asch Mezareph, the book of the Jew Abraham and of Nicholas Flamel, restored, translated, and annotated by Éliphas Lévi."[141] The mysterious manuscript, in which all texts are jumbled together, is printed in the supplement (407ff.) to *La Clef des Grand Mystères* (Paris, 1860) by Éliphas Lévi (Alphonse Louis Constant, 1810–1875) and was dreamed up as a "rediscovered" text of the *Esh Meẓaref,* whereby the great mystagogue, who today still has his readers, proves himself to be a true descendant of the old alchemical-mystical pseudoepigraphy.

Thus Knorr von Rosenroth was able to allude to this function of the Kabbalah as mystical alchemy in a verse of the Latin dedication, which prefaces his book in the form of an explanation of the allegorical frontispiece:

> *Alterat abstrusos minerarum in corde meatus.*
> (It changes the abstruse course of the minerals
> in the heart.)

---

141 J.K. Huysmans, *Down There* (New York, 1972), 76.

Little is known of Jewish alchemy after the composition of the *Esh Meẓaref,* and even less of any connection to kabbalist ideas. We have already dealt with Moroccan alchemy. Here and there one finds alchemical recipes for making gold or for "coloring" metals in later manuscripts, especially in collectanea of so-called "practical Kabbalah," a term that in the Hebrew parlance means nothing other than magic. The authenticity of a report about an adept in Hamburg named Benjamin Jesse is highly dubious. An anonymous informant who claimed to have been taken into Jesse's home from a foundling hospital reports that Jesse lived so solitarily that no one knew of him. When he died in 1730 at the age of eighty-eight, his adopted son received a handsome bequest, while the remaining assets went to two cousins in Switzerland. Among those were a can of weighty scarlet-colored powder (scrapings from the Philosopher's Stone) and something comparatively less valuable, namely, four large crates filled with gold bullion. Kopp, who read this report, rightly assumes this to be a fictitious tease to make the mouths of the alchemists water.[142] The report also gives an accounting of the adept's last day, including his reciting Hebrew psalms and drinking a little Malvasia wine shortly before his death. There is, however, no Benjamin Jesse buried in the old Jewish cemetery in Hamburg.[143]

In contrast to this was Samuel Jacob Ḥayyim Falk, widely renowned in his time as Dr. Falk and even more famous under the moniker "Ba'al Shem of London."[144] Falk was born either in Fürth, Germany, or in Podhajce, Ukraine, around 1708 and died in London in 1782. The numerous contempo-

---

142 Kopp, op. cit., vol. 1, 95.

143 It is not listed in M. Grunwald's book *Hamburgs deutsche Juden bis 1811* (Hamburg, 1904), who based his research on old gravestones, especially those of the cemetery of Ottensen.

144 Cf. H. Adler in *Transactions of the Jewish Historical Society of England,* vol. 5 (1908), 148–73; as well as C. Roth, *Essays and Portraits in Anglo-Jewish History* (Philadelphia, 1962), 139–64.

rary reports and polemics on him can be amended and veri-
fied by his own manuscripts and the diary of his *famulus*.[145]
It seems certain that he was, at the same time, a kabbalist,
a practicing magician, and an alchemist, but about his alchemical practices we have the least concrete material. For
one, there is the independent testimony of his disciple Rabbi
Tobia ben Jehuda from the Cracow region, who in 1773 told
the Hebraist and diarist Ezra Stiles at Yale University that
he himself had seen the Philosopher's Stone and the transmutation of metals.[146] That Stiles's conversational partner
came indeed from London, where he might have seen such
practices at Dr. Falk's, is authenticated. As esteemed as the
Ba'al Shem of London was in non-Jewish circles, even within
the aristocracy, as controversial was his reputation among
the Jews. It was tainted not only by the dark aura of magic
but by the even darker (presumably not baseless) accusa-
tions of being a crypto-Shabbethaian. When he died in 1782,
the epitaph on his grave praised him as "an accomplished
sage, an adept in Cabbalah."[147] The famous Jerusalem emis-
sary and eminent scholar Ḥayyim Joseph Azoulai, however,
spoke out against him with profound disapproval when the
highborn Marchesa de Croix told him in Paris that she, a
non-Jewess, was taught practical Kabbalah by Falk. Consid-
erably more dubious was the reputation of three men who
practiced alchemy in the last quarter of the eighteenth
century. The first one was Jacob Frank, the founder of the

---

145 In the Adler collection at New York Theological Seminary and
the library of the London Beth Din. Cf. A. Neubauer, *Catalogue of the
Hebrew Manuscript in the Jews' College* (London and Oxford, 1886), nos.
127–30, 27.

146 See A. Chiel, in *Studies in Jewish Bibliography, History and Literature, in Honor of Edward Kiev* (New York, 1971), 85–89.

147 N.H. Webster, *Secret Societies and Subversive Movements* (London, 1924), 188.

Frankist sect, about whom I have written elsewhere.[148]
We know that he set up alchemical laboratories, first in
Brünn and later in Offenbach, and that he referred to al-
chemy several times in his "instructions" to his disciples.[149]
To the outside world, however, Frank and his nephew Moses
Dobruška, whose alchemical activities cannot be doubted,
were feigned Catholics. Dobruška, who converted to the
Catholic faith in 1773, was elevated to nobility in Vienna in
1778 as Franz Thomas Edler von Schönfeld.[150]

Together with Ephraim Joseph Hirschfeld,[151] who did not
convert, Dobruška became one of the main conspirators of
the "Knights of St. John the Evangelists for Asia in Europe,"
a secret society of freemasons that was much talked about
in Germany and Austria between 1783 and 1790, not least
because it was the first German-speaking fraternal order to
accept Jews.[152] The writings of these "Asiatic Brethren," as
they were commonly called, some published in print, leave
no doubt about the alchemical tendencies of the group.
They did not derive, however, from Jewish kabbalist tradition but are connected with the Rosicrucianism of the late

---

148 G. Scholem, "The Holiness of Sin," *Commentary* 51 (January 1971),
68; "Redemption through Sin," in *The Messianic Idea in Judaism and
Other Essays on Jewish Spirituality* (New York, 1971); "Jacob Frank and
the Frankists," in G. Scholem, *Kabbalah* (New York, 1987).

149 Jacob Frank is supposed to have had such a laboratory, as is
documented in the second volume of A. Kraus, *Frank i Frankiści polscy*
(Cracow, 1895), 73. Frank speaks in several places of his "Book of
Words of the Lord" about alchemy, which is preserved in a Polish autograph, e.g., in par. 254: "Just as the entire world seeks and wishes to
make gold, so I wish to transmute you to refined gold."

150 On Dobruška, see G. Scholem, *Du Frankisme au Jacobinisme: La
vie de Moses Dobruška alias Franz Thomas von Schönfeld alias Junius Frey*,
trans. N. Deutsch (Paris, 1981).

151 On Hirschfeld, see my essay in the *Yearbook of the Leo Baeck
Institute* 7 (London, 1962), 247–78.

152 Cf. J. Katz, *Jews and Freemasons* (Cambridge, 1970), 26–53.

eighteenth century, about which I will speak below. There is no doubt that beyond their rather modest alchemical proclivities, these four men also had kabbalist, or rather heretic-kabbalist, convictions; but from a Jewish perspective, they were clearly mere marginal figures at or beyond the boundaries of Jewish tradition.

An alchemist's laboratory as pictured in Heinrich Khunrath's
Amphitheatrum Sapientiae Æternae (Hamburg, 1595)

III

In concluding this study, I will return to the initial question of how alchemy and Kabbalah became widely synonymous among the Christian theosophers and alchemists of Europe, and the impact of this process of identification on its literature.

Two elements were primarily responsible for this questionable transition from the Kabbalah to alchemy, as it occurred after 1500 and particularly after 1600. There is a third element, the market criers, which I am setting aside here, without minimizing their influence. To them apply the words of H. Kopp in reference to certain types of alchemical-kabbalist works: "Here … Kabbalah was only the bait, mostly already employed in the titles, to lure curious readers into buying books by authors who knew nothing about this sort of occult knowledge."[153] It is difficult to ascertain from Kopp's somewhat ironic remarks, made after the publication of the *Kabbala Denudata,* whether he felt there were other elements that contributed to a *true* connection between alchemy and Kabbalah. In any case, the following comments will pursue a different course.

One could say that Pico della Mirandola's sensational thesis, duly condemned by the pope, that Kabbalah and magic were "two sciences that more than any other prove the divine nature of Christ" was the starting point for this identification of Kabbalah with other disciplines. In the case of

---

153 Kopp, op. cit., vol. 2, 232.

Pico, it was a matter of introducing Kabbalah into the symbolic world of the Florentine circle around Marsilio Ficino and their pursuit of a religion and tradition common to all mankind. For Pico and his followers, such as Johannes Reuchlin, Cardinal Egidio da Viterbo, the Franciscan Francisco Giorgio, and the learned convert Paulo Riccio, it was not yet about alchemy. But the two elements essential to this process of transition did indeed originate, if not yet in systematic form, in his writings, namely, in the Christian reinterpretation of Kabbalah and magic, as he understood it. The natural magic of the sixteenth century, which was based primarily on the *Occulta Philosophia* of Agrippa of Nettesheim, is of course already far removed from Pico's concept of magic. It instead absorbed medieval aspects of angelology, demonology, and necromancy. In his great work, which was intended to integrate all the occult sciences, Agrippa, influenced by Reuchlin's two books on the subject of Kabbalah,[154] identified Kabbalah largely with magic. He adopted certain elements of speculative Kabbalah that fit into his occult system, sometimes making highly incorrect associations, as in book 3, chapter 10, in regard to the relation of the seven *sefirot* to the metals. Agrippa did not possess an indepth knowledge of the kabbalist teachings and symbolism, but he stood his ground, welding together Jewish-Medieval and Christian angelology and demonology. Every one of his faithful disciples, and there was no shortage of them, could characterize the neo-Pythagorean nature symbolism, in good conscious, as kabbalist.

It should not come as a surprise that soon after Agrippa, especially in the second half of the sixteenth century, there was a stream of novel cosmological and cosmogonic ideas, most of them derived from scholarly speculation and the ex-

---

154 *De Verbo Mirifico* (Basel, 1494) and *De Arte Cabalistica* (Hagenau, 1517).

isting framework of natural magic.[155] In the area of alchemy, the influence of Agrippa is especially reflected in Steffan Michelspacher's *Cabala sive speculum artis et naturæ in alchymia* (Augsburg, 1616, reprinted several times). Its "alchemical-kabbalist" tables have nothing to do with Jewish Kabbalah. It should also be noted that the notion of Kabbalah as the lowest kind of magic art has to be attributed to Agrippa as well. When Agrippa's learned magic lost its credibility in the scholarly world, it entered the lower social groups, naturally much simplified – or rather brutalized, and thus still continues to play a role to this day in Western magic literature, often glorified as Kabbalah. These are the connections that have emerged most vividly from the research on the Faust myth and Faustian magic books.[156]

The relationship of natural magic to Kabbalah, which lacks any alchemical momentum, can be determined quite precisely, but I cannot explain the relationship of Paracelsus to the connection of alchemy, magic, and Kabbalah based on my own studies. The ambiguous position of the most important occultist of the sixteenth century on Kabbalah, which Paracelsus knew from Reuchlin's and Agrippa's writings, requires its own study, for which I do not have the necessary resources here in Jerusalem, in particular, the large critical edition by K. Sudhoff. Two major works by Peuckert that deal in depth with Agrippa, Paracelsus, and their disciples, *Pansophie* (1936) and *Gabalia* (1967), leave me at a loss on the question of Paracelsus's position. I am hopeful that some other critically inclined scholar will one day tackle this complex problem.

Twenty years ago a friend and I paid an unforgettable visit to the wonderful mystical library of Oskar Schlag in Zurich,

---

155 Described in detail in W.-E. Peuckert, *Pansophie* (Stuttgart, 1936); cf. also F. Secret, *Les kabbalists chrétiens de la renaissance* (Paris, 1964).

156 See primarily C. Kiesewetter, *Faust in der Geschichte und Tradition* (Leipzig, 1893), especially vol. 2.

where I pulled from the shelf a volume of the Sudhoff edition of Paracelsus's works. My eye immediately fell upon a sentence that began with the words: "The devil, the great Cabalist that he is." Was it a coincidence? Much later I learned that Paracelsus differentiated between a devilish and a divine Kabbalah; one he condemned, the other he raised heavenward.

From the equivalence of experimental magic with Kabbalah in Agrippa and his school, the alchemists eventually drew the conclusion that the natural, experimental, yet occult processes of alchemy could also fall under the collective term of Kabbalah. Similarly, the more mystically and theologically disposed among them could use the "Christian Kabbalah" for the identification of both heterogeneous disciplines. The expression "Christian Kabbalah" is not yet used by its first representatives named above. It first surfaces as the title of a didactic poem by the Franciscan Jean Thenaud, *La Saincte et trescrestienne cabale* that, though dedicated to King Francis I of France, did not appear in print until our time.[157] In the numerous printed texts of that kind from the sixteenth century, this terminology is missing, as is, by the way, any clear connection to alchemy.

The definitive blending of these elements emerges most assertively in the large folio of Heinrich Khunrath of Leipzig (1560–1605), at the time a famous alchemist and mystic. Titled *Amphitheatrum sapientæ æternæ solius veræ, christiano-Kabalisticum, divino-magicum nec non physico-chymicum ter-trinuum catholicum* (Hanover, 1609), it emphatically argues for this identification process. The verbose author revels in the pictorial world of the disciplines listed by him on the title page. His ideas of what constitutes kabbalism are evidently determined by a compendium published by Johann Nidanus Pistorius, *Artis Cabalisticæ* (Basel, 1587), a folio of

---

157 Cf. J.L. Blau, *The Christian Interpretation of the Cabala in the Renaissance* (New York, 1944), 89–98, 121–44.

nearly a thousand pages in which two authentic texts of Kabbalah are grouped with Christian-kabbalist writings by Pico, Reuchlin, Riccio, the Franciscan Archangelus de Burgonovo, and the popular *Dialoghi di amore* by Leo Hebræus (Judah Abrabanel). All this heterogeneous material, which has nothing or very little to with the authentic Kabbalah, is accepted by Pistorius as kabbalist without, as far as I can see, naming any sources. Khunrath's interest in alchemy, especially if mystically understood, was overwhelming and forms the theme for his earlier writings. In one of them, which was distributed widely, he treats the rich symbolism of the "hylic chaos" as the *prima materia* of alchemy and thus contributes to the analogy made between God's seven-day work of the Creation and the respective stages of the Great Work of the alchemists.[158] The full-page allegorical engravings of Khunrath's work, which were published separately several years earlier, were considered in alchemist and theosophist circles as important representations of Kabbalah.[159] These engravings also fell into the hands of Jacob ben Ḥayyim Ẓemaḥ, the famous kabbalist of the Lurian school, apparently while he was still in his crypto-Jewish Marrano period in Spain (before he openly converted back to Judaism in Salonica). He makes fun of it in one of his polemical writings against falsifications of the Christian Kabbalah. He does not mention Khunrath by name, but his description leaves no doubt about the identity of his source.[160]

---

158 Khunrath's book, *Vom hylischen Chaos,* was published in German in 1597 and in Latin a year later. I was not able to inspect it until 1978 in The Hague.

159 This engraving was printed separately after 1602. Khunrath's posthumously published *De Igne Magorum* (Strasbourg, 1608) included as an addendum an anonymous "Report of a Cabalist about the 4 Figures of the Great Amphitheatri Khunradi." I have not yet seen this report.

160 I published Ẓemaḥ's polemics against this engraving in *Kirjath Sepher* 27 (1951), 108.

The highly regarded *Lexicon Alchemiæ* by the Paracelsus disciple Martin Ruland, [161] published shortly after Khunrath's work, was rather cautious in its judgment, while in the following decades, Khunrath's identification was almost taken for granted. Another identification of Kabbalah with alchemy, dating from around Khunrath's time, occurred in the interpolations of Pierre Arnauld de la Chevallerie, which was inserted into his first edition of Nicholas Flamel's *Livre des figures hieroglyphiques* (Paris, 1612). Describing the folios of the alleged papyrus book, which Flamel had discovered, Arnauld put the words into Flamel's mouth that no one would be able to understand alchemy without having an advanced knowledge of their (e.g., the Jews') traditional Kabbalah *(Cabale traditive)* and assiduously studying its books, even though the work of alchemy is introduced here with great diligence and skill. [162]

Around the same time, the Paracelsus disciple Franz Kieser, who had knowledge of Khunrath's unpublished writings, combined Kabbalah and alchemy in a similar way. He published a kind of distillation of Paracelsus's doctrines, *Cabala chymica* (Frankfurt, 1606), in which it says that magic is the philosophy of the alchemists and "belonging to this, a preferred part of the Kabbalah," true to Paracelsus, distinguishing, of course, between a devilish, corrupt Kabbalah and an unflawed one, which is none other than the highest completion of true philosophy. In the same book he declares, like Flamel's interpolator and, later, Thomas Vaughan: "It can clearly be assumed that no one will attain the *summa arcani* (the sum of all secrets) in eternity, unless he is experienced in magic and Kabbalah." This comes very close to Khunrath's

---

161 *Lexicon Alchemiæ* (Frankfurt, 1612), 295ff.

162 F. Secret pointed out this interpolation in *Bibliothèque d'Humanisme et Renaissance* 35 (1973), 104. On Flamel, see Waite, *The Secret Tradition in Alchemy*, 137–62.

sentence that "Kabbalah, magic, and alchemy shall and must be combined and used together." [163]

The mystical conception of alchemy found its most influential expression, shortly after, in the writings by the so-called Rosicrucians, which began to be published in 1614, especially the *Chymische Hochzeit Christiani Rosencreutz*, which today is acknowledged to be authored by the Swabian theologist and theosophist Johann Valentin Andreæ (1586–1654) who, as an enthusiastic youth, had dreamed of a mystical reformation of Christianity. Whether or not there existed a true Rosicrucian brotherhood prior to the eighteenth century is irrelevant to our purposes; however, some of the arguments provoked by these early Rosicrucian writings are significant here because of their lasting effect.

Especially important for establishing the wide recognition of the link between Christian Kabbalah and alchemy and magic were the English theosophers, who actively participated in these debates and exerted enormous influence on the organization of Rosicrucianism in the eighteenth century. I am thinking here of Thomas Vaughan (1641–1666) and the slightly older Robert Fludd (1574–1637). The equivalence of kabbalist and alchemical symbols is pervasive in several of Fludd's writings, whereby, of course, the making of gold is only a material symbol for the transmutation of mankind toward the stage of perfection in Christ. In Fludd's tractate *Truth's Golden Harrow* (written around 1625) [164] and in his last major book, *Philosophia Moysaica* (1638), one finds – in a kabbalist symbolism of the two forms of the letter *alef* – the alchemical transmutation of the dark *prima materia* into the brightly shining Stone of Wisdom. In his explanation of the Hebrew alphabet, Jacob ha-Kohen, a thirteenth-century Spanish kabbalist from Soria,

---

163 *De Igne Magorum*, new ed., 75.

164 Fludd's tractate *Truth's Golden Harrow* was published by C.H. Josten in *Ambix* 3 (1949), 91–150.

distinguishes between a dark, external form of the letters and a lighter, mystical one, symbolized on the parchment of the Torah by the white (blank) space between the black-inked shapes. Reuchlin, who had read this tractate in a kabbalist manuscript, prompted Fludd to adopt this alchemical reinterpretation, which appears frequently in the latter's writings. According to Fludd, the precious stones on the breastplate of the high priest, which had already been interpreted mystically by the kabbalists as lights – called in the Torah *Urim v'Tumim* (the shining letters of the oracle), although its original meaning is no longer clear – allude to the process of transformation of the "stones" into the Stone of Wisdom, which is just this *Urim*. Thus, in addition to images from many other sources, alchemical interpretations of biblical verses and kabbalist motives, probably going back to Pistorius, pervade Fludd's writings.

The same may be said about the tractates of Thomas Vaughan, which were still being read in the eighteenth century and which always combined and related both symbolic worlds. In his *Magia Adamica,* Vaughan states explicitly that the Kabbalah of the Jews is "chimicall" and expresses itself in natural events, referring, however, to his source as the fictitious book of the Jew Abraham, whose revelations were based on Nicholas Flamel. These texts were all written about 25 to 50 years prior to the publication of the *Kabbala Denudata.* It is only natural that kindred spirits such as these authors would find in Knorr von Rosenroth's work the confirmation of their long-fostered opinion on the harmony, if not identity, between alchemy and Kabbalah. But even two years after the first volume of the *Kabbala Denudata* (which includes the *Esh Meẓaref*), the *Coelum Sephiroticum Hebræorum* by Johann Christophorus Steeb (Mainz, 1679) makes no reference to these new developments; and the sky of the *sefirot* is here described exclusively by the means provided by Agrippa and the compendium of Pistorius, with medicine and natural science, and embellished with alchemy.

I am unable to say when the use of the two intersecting triangles of the hexagram were adopted by alchemists as a symbol for the alchemical connection of fire and water. It has been explained with the Midrashic interpretation of the Hebrew word for sky, *shamayim*, as a combination of *esh* (fire) and *mayim* (water). In any case, around 1720 the symbol was already popular in alchemy. Peuckert cites the hexagram in the circle as a magic sign used by Jews, allegedly in necromancy, whereby he refers to Paracelsus but concedes in his notes that the respective drawing exists only in a handwritten marginalia in a copy of Huser's edition of Paracelsus's writings, which Peuckert used in Wrocław.[165] Magical hexagrams appeared, of course, in Jewish amulets, albeit not exclusively so, as the "Seal of Solomon" and later as the "Shield of David." Surely this Jewish terminology was known to the alchemical author who in 1724 published in Berleburg, a famous center of Christian theosophy, a booklet titled *Naturæ Naturantis & Naturatæ Mysterium in Scuto Davidico exhibitum.*

At the conclusion of this development stand two Southern German theosophists in whose writings Kabbalah and alchemy are joined in a kind of intimate union, the formation of which I have been trying to describe. Both were markedly mystical spirits who sought to unfold a universal symbolism.

---

165 Cf. W.-E. Peuckert, *Pansophie*, 245, where the pentacle and the hexagram are depicted inside a double circle, characters that Paracelsus says were still "highly concealed [among some Jews], for they accomplish everything, break all evil spells, are mighty against the devil and more valuable than all figures, pentacula, sigilla Salomonis, because it is used in the name of the most Supreme." The contradiction between this sentence and the two drawings is apparent. From the inscriptions, it is evident that they are in fact not Jewish, but rather of Christian origin. The pentacle is inscribed not only in Latin letters, with the Greek denotation for the name of God, *tetragrammaton,* but also with the name of Jesus in the older spelling, Jhsus; the hexagram is inscribed in Latin with the names of Adonai and Jeova – all obviously incompatible with Judaism.

They are Georg von Welling (1652–1727) and the Swabian prelate and theosopher Friedrich Christoph Oetinger (1702–1782), both men of great influence on their generation and the one succeeding them. Welling's main work fully discloses its nature on the title page. It was first published completely as *Opus Mago-Cabbalisticum et Theosophicum, Including (therein) the Origin, Nature, Characteristics and Usage of Salt, Sulphur and Mercury Described In Three Parts, and Among Several Odd Mathematic, Theosophic, Magic and Mystic Materials, the Production of Metals and Minerals on the Ground of Nature Will Be Illustrated, Including the Main Key To the Work As a Whole, and Various Strange Mago-Kabbalistic Figures. In Addition, There Will Be Provided: A Treatise On Divine Wisdom and a Special Appendix of a Number of Very Rare and Precious Chemical Ingredients.* This book was lying on Goethe's desk at the time he joined the circle of Susanna von Klettenberg, and Goethe also describes it in the second part of *Poetry and Truth*. The intention of Welling was essentially the same as that of Paracelsus, who was resolved to relate the two lights – the light of grace and the light of nature – and demonstrate therein their efficacy. As Welling says in the preface, his ambition is not to teach physical alchemy, "the making of gold but rather it is directed at something much higher, namely, how nature can be seen in God and how God can be recognized in the same and how furthermore from this wisdom the true service of the creature as an owed thank offering emanates toward the Creator." The voluminous book is dominated by theosophically reinterpreted alchemical ideas but also interwoven with concepts by the mago-kabbalists, whereby a total amalgamation of these two areas is achieved. The expression "Mago-Kabbalah" reflects the continually evolving intertwining of magic and Kabbalah that has occurred since Pico and which can be found in all previously encountered texts, and also in Jacob Boehme. Without a doubt, Welling, who was highly educated and literate, adopted some Jewish-kabbalist ideas and also was well acquainted with Knorr von Rosenroth's

Kabbala Denudata. Essentially, however, his notion of Kabbalah is not that different from Paracelsus and his school and thus relates to Jewish tradition in name only.

The fundamental myth that forms the starting point of Welling's work (especially in the first chapter on salt and the seven-day work of Creation) and was adopted later by many others, is foreign to kabbalist tradition. It is an original version of the revolt of Lucifer at the beginning of the Creation, which derives from the Jewish apocalypse (the Book of Enoch) and was further expanded by the Gnostics. Welling's basic thoughts in this regard have rightly been called a "cosmic history myth." [166] "At the beginning there was the world of light of God and the spirits, at the center of which stood Lucifer, reflecting the divine as the first and most magnificent of God's creatures. But Lucifer's will inhibited the effect of the divine light." Thus in his sphere arose a space of chaos, of darkness and gravity, from which God created the solar system. While reveling in the consciousness and appreciation of the encompassing glory, Lucifer had in fact forgotten his origin and therefore, by developing his own will, sequestered himself from God. According to God's plan, it was Adam, not Lucifer, who was supposed to be "in his image and dominate the earth." But Adam turned away from God in his Fall, and this results in the battle between Lucifer's forces and those of God in the Creation and humankind itself. Only at the end of days will God's interfering fire of strength transform the world, restore God's world of light, and return all beings, eventually even Lucifer, to their original harmonic, pre-dialectical state. Thus each of Paracelsus's three basic alchemical elements – salt, sulphur, and mercury – have a special relation to one of the epochs of salvific history: salt to God's world of lights, the Fall of Lucifer, and the Creation of the world; sulphur to the balm of life of all

---

166 Cf. E. Trunz in *Goethe's Werke* (Hamburg, 1955), vol. 9, 717, whose excellent summary I am following here.

creatures, but also to the destroying fire, which determines the state of humans after death and the end of days in the Last Judgment; and mercury to the bringing back of all things in the eon of the new heavens and the new earth.

A Jewish-Haggadic element that derived from the mago-kabbalists but was not necessarily kabbalist is very significant for Welling. In the *esh-mayim,* the "fiery water," which precedes the Creation of the world, the three elements are combined. Welling represents this union with a circle inscribed with a hexagram, just as for the alchemists the two intersecting triangles were used as symbols for the elements water and fire. Thus although Welling was probably unaware of it, it was through him that the figure of the Jewish Shield of David acquired the symbolism of perfection in many alchemical and Rosicrucian texts of the eighteenth century.

Of course, Welling also mentions authentic kabbalist ideas such as the speculations on the *sefirot,* through which the "Hebraic mago-kabbalists" point out the different effects of the Godhead on the spirits, angels, and earthly creatures.[167] It is precisely from this that he breaks away, however, most decisively. This shows how little his book could have been a source for the knowledge of Jewish Kabbalah and how here everything was becoming Christian (and alchemical-mystical). He wrote (208):

> Solely because we never could rhyme together all these mysteries and wonderful allocations with the truth of the Holy Scriptures, indeed also not have any reason to do so, because they [the Jews] do not recognize the Revelation of the Divine Majesty's

---

167 Whenever Welling cites the mago-kabbalists, they are not authentic kabbalist phrases, as far as I was able to ascertain. They seem rather like quotations from Paracelsus or related literature. It would be interesting to determine his sources.

Fiat ... [168] Their Kabbalah is such that one cannot force anything from it; but he who knows how to combine all the pieces of the New Testament with the Old [Testament], has learned the correct Kabbalah perfectly ... The Jewish Kabbalah is nothing other than an abuse of divine names.

With this deformation or transformation, if not transmutation, of the Jewish Kabbalah into something purely Christian, and thus more accessible for the alchemical reinterpretation, we have reached the end of the process that has occupied us here.

So influential was Welling's book that it was used as a main source of ideas in the formation of freemasonry around 1780. Both the didactic publications of the masonic circle of Golden and Rosy Cross and those of the Asiatic Brethren, which partially originated in the same circle but distanced themselves polemically from it, adopted Welling's Luficer myth almost verbatim. Astonishingly, in the writings of the Asiatic Brethren, pseudo-kabbalist mythology and authentic kabbalist tradition joined together on the subject of the beginnings of Creation, albeit one that derived from the heretic circle of the later adherents of Sabbatai Sevi.

The authentic connection of Jewish Kabbalah with an alchemistic-mystical symbolism of Christian character that was finally adopted by Friedrich Christoph Oetinger derived from theology and from published, Christian-interpreted excerpts of the Zohar. [169] Jacob Boehme, who developed a kabbalist symbolism of his own, was brought to Oetinger's attention by

---

168 Welling seems to understand under *Fiat* the divinity of Christ, alluded to in Genesis 1:3, which is not recognized by Jews.

169 Oetinger primarily used the collection of Gottfried Christoph Sommer, *Theologiæ Soharicæ cum Christiana Amice Convenientis* (Gotha, 1734).

the Frankfurt kabbalist Koppel Hecht.[170] It is not necessary
to discuss this chapter further here since we now have two
excellent studies on the prehistory of kabbalist traditions in
Swabian theology of the seventeenth century and the kabbalist and alchemical symbolism in Oetinger by F. Häussermann,
who delved deeply into these subjects.[171]

170 Hecht died young, in December 1729. In the spring of that
year, Oetinger had paid him a visit.

171 Häussermann's studies, "Pictura Docens" and "Theologia Em-
blematica," were published in *Blätter für Württembergische Kirchenge-
schichte* (1966–67), 65–153; (1968–69), 207–346; (1972), 71–112. These
studies are among the best published to date on the Christian Kabbalah of the seventeenth and eighteenth centuries.

Opening page of the *Sefer ha-Ikkarim* by Joseph Albo
(Italy, end of the 15th century)

INDEX

GERSHOM SCHOLEM (1897–1982) was a noted authority on Jewish mysticism. His books include *Major Trends in Jewish Mysticism, Kabbalah, On the Mystical Shape of the Godhead, Sabbatai Sevi: the Mystical Messiah, On the Kabbalah and Its Symbolism,* and *Origins of the Kabbalah.*

KLAUS OTTMANN previously translated Gershom Scholem's essay on "Colors and their Symbolism in Jewish Tradition and Mysticism" for the new, expanded edition of *Color Symbolism: The Eranos Lectures.* He is also the author of *The Genius Decision: The Extraordinary and the Postmodern Condition* and *Thought Through My Eyes: Writings on Art, 1977–2005,* and has recently translated *Overcoming the Problematics of Art: The Writings of Yves Klein.*